MASTERS OF MUSIC

THE HISTORY OF ROCK MUSIC

TEXT BY:
ANDREA BERGAMINI

ILLUSTRATIONS BY:

STUDIO L.R. GALANTE, MANUELA CAPPON, L.R. GALANTE, ALESSANDRO MENCHI, FRANCESCO SPADONI, IVAN STALIO

BARRON'S

DoGi

English Translation
© Copyright 2000 by
Barron's Educational
Series, Inc.
Original Edition © 1999 by
DoGi spa, Florence, Italy
Title of original edition:
Il rock e la sua storia
Italian edition by:
Andrea Bergamini
Illustrations:
Studio L.R. Galante:
*Manuela Cappon,
L.R. Galante,
Alessandro Menchi,
Francesco Spadoni;*
Andrea Ricciardi,
Ivan Stalio
Editor:
Andrea Bachini
Graphic Display:
Tommaso Gomez
Art Director and
Page make up:
Sebastiano Ranchetti

Translation from Italian by:
Marion Lignana Rosenberg

Barron's Educational Series, Inc.
250 Wireless Boulevard
Hauppauge, NY 11788
http://www.barronseduc.com

Library of Congress Catalog
Card No. 99-66546

International Standard Book No.
0-7641-5137-1

Printed in Italy
9 8 7 6 5 4 3 2 1

HOW TO READ THIS BOOK

Each two-page spread makes up a chapter on the background, leading figures, musical instruments, and great moments of rock history. From time to time, a spread covers the different historical and social events that had an impact on rock music. The text on the upper left (1) and the large central image are devoted to the main theme. The other elements, including photos and portraits, round out the presentation.

ACKNOWLEDGMENTS

ABBREVIATIONS: *t* top; *b* bottom; *c* center; *r* right; *l* left.

ILLUSTRATIONS:
The original, previously unpublished illustrations in this volume were created by order and under the supervision of DoGi spa, who is the copyright holder.
CREDITS: Manuela Cappon: 28–29, 30–31, 32–33, 44–45, 48–49; L.R. Galante: 10–11, 16–17, 18–19, 38–39, 60–61; Alessandro Menchi: 14–15, 36–37, 40–41, 56–57, 58–59; Andrea Ricciardi: 4–5, 6–7; Francesco Spadoni: 12–13, 34–35, 46–47, 50–51, 54–55; Ivan Stalio: 8–9, 20–21, 22–23, 24–25, 26–27, 42–43, 52–53.

FRONTISPIECE: L.R.Galante.
COVER: Ivan Stalio; Sebastiano Ranchetti (computer elaboration)

LIST OF REPRODUCTIONS:
DoGi spa has made every attempt to contact possible copyright holders and apologizes for any errors or omissions, which it will be happy to correct in subsequent editions of this work.
(Works reproduced in their entirety are followed by the letter e; those from which only a detail is shown are followed by the letter d.)
6. *Senator Joseph McCarthy, Life Magazine* photo, 1954 d; **7.** *Doris Day* (ACE Archive) d; **8l.** Cover of a U.S. edition of *The Catcher in the Rye* (DoGi Archive, Florence) e; **8r.** *Drive in* (photo by Winston Link) e; **9.** *Bathing Suit Advertisement* by Peter Hawley, 1951 e; **10.** *Muddy Waters* (photo by Norbert Hess) d; **11l.** *Anonymous Cover of a Record by Fats Domino* (Antinea Photo) e; **11r.** Cover of *Beyond the Sunset* by Hank Williams (ACE Archive) e; **12r.** *Jukebox* (IGDA Archive, Milan) e; **12d.** Cover of *Rockin' the Joint* by Bill Haley (Sunset Boulevard / Boyer) e; **13l.** *African-American Gatherings* (Associated Press Photo) e; **13r.** *A 1950's Radio* (Robert Ellis / Repfoto) e; **14.** *Chuck Berry* (Grazia Neri, Milan) e; **15.** *Pat Boone* (IGDA Archive) d; **16tl.** *A Sun Records Disc* (BMI Records) e; **16c.** Cover of "Hound Dog" / "Don't Be Cruel" by Elvis Presley (RCA Victor) e; **16b.** Poster for Elvis Presley's Film *Love Me Tender* (CinemaScope Picture) e; **17t.** *Colonel Parker* (Associated Press Photo) d; **17b.** *Elvis's Fans* (Associated Press Photo) d; **18tl.** *Jerry Lee Lewis* (IGDA Archive, Milan) d; **18tr.** *A Houston Baptist Church* (K. Bernstein / Contrasto); **18br.** *Carl Lee Perkins* (IGDA Archive, Milan) e; **20tl.** *Buddy Holly* (IGDA Archive, Milan) d; **20tr.** *Dick Clark* (John Topham Picture Library) e; **20b.** *The Twist* (Corbis-Bettman / UPI Photo) e; **21tr.** *Alan Freed* (John Topham Picture Library) d; **22t.** *Woody Guthrie* (IGDA Archive, Milan) d; **22b.** *The Byrds* (Sony Music Entertainment Inc.) e; **23tc.** *A Street in Greenwich Village, New York* (IGDA Archive, Milan) e; **23tr.** *Bob Dylan with an Electric Guitar* (Giovanni Canitano Photo) d; **24t.** Cover of the Beatles' Album *Please Please Me* (DoGi Archive, Florence) e; **25tr.** *Gerry and the Pacemakers* (IGDA Archive, Milan) e; **26.** *A London Suburb* (Touring Club Italiano, Milano) d; **27tl.** *John Lennon* (EMI Archives, London); **27tr.** *Mini Morris* (Rover Morris Historical Archives) e; **27bl.** Victor de Vasarely, *Kalota*, 1963 (Pace Gallery, New York) e; **28tl.** Cover of the Rolling Stones' Album *Around and Around* (Decca Records) e; **28bl.** *Keith Richards and Mick Jagger* (ACE Archive); **29tc.** Photo of Neil Shafton from the album *I Don't Want to Know You* e; **29r.** *The Who* (Polygram) e; **29b.** Cover of the English edition of *A Clockwork Orange* (Robert Ellis / Repfoto) e; **30tl.** *The Supremes* (David Behl Photo, New York) e; **30b.** *Aretha Franklin* (DoGi Archive, Florence) d; **31tl.** *John Kennedy* (DoGi Archive, Florence) d; **31tr.** *Otis Redding* (DoGi Archive, Florence) d; **32.** *Hippie* (DoGi Archive, Florence) d; **33tc.** *Beach Boys*

(Robert Ellis / Repfoto) d; **33tr.** *Poster for a Psychedelic Concert* (La Repubblica) e; **33br.** *Poster for the Jefferson Airplane* (La Repubblica) e; **34tl.** Cover of the Beatles' Record "Strawberry Fields Forever / Penny Lane" (Parlophone Records) e; **34tr.** *An LP* (DoGi Archive, Florence) d; **35tr.** Cover of the Beatles' Album *Sergeant Pepper* (EMI Records, Hayes Middlesex, England) e; **35b.** *John Lennon and Yoko Ono* (The David Jeffen Company); **36t.** *Lou Reed* (RCA Records) e; **36c.** Andy Warhol, *Yellow Banana*, cover for the Velvet Underground & Nico's Album of the Same Name (ACE Archive) e; **37tl.** *Jack Kerouac* (Grazia Neri, Milan) d; **37tr.** *Frank Zappa* (Giovanni Canitano Photo) d; **38tl.** *Program for the Woodstock Festival*, New York (Gallimard) e; **38tr.** *Janis Joplin* (Associated Press Photo) d; **38b.** *Jim Morrison* (Associated Press Photo) d; **39.** *Poster for the Isle of Wight Rock Festival* (Popperfoto) e; **40tl.** *Lyndon B. Johnson* (USAF Archives) d; **40tr.** *The Rolling Stones in Altamont* 1969 (Decca Archives, London) d; **40b.** *Clash at Kent State University* (Könemann) d; **41t.** *Malcolm X* (Eve Arnold Photo / Magnum / Agenzia Contrasto, Rome) e; **41b.** *Martin Luther King* (Könemann) d; **42.** *Cream* (DoGi Archive, Florence) d; **43tc.** *Jimi Hendrix's Funeral* (Associated Press Photo) d; **43tr.** *Leo Fender* (Leo Fender Archive) d; **43c.** *Hendrix at Woodstock* (Atlantic / Universal, London) d; **44.** *David Bowie Dressed as Ziggy Stardust* (RCA Limited) d; **45.** *Cover of Black Sabbath's Album Black Sabbath* (Warner Bros. Records Inc.) e; **46l.** *Joni Mitchell* (Giovanni Canitano Photo) d; **46r.** *Jackson Browne* (Giovanni Canitano Photo) d; **47tl.** *Robert De Niro in Taxi Driver* (Columbia Pictures) e; **48.** Cover of Genesis' Album *Fox Trot* (ACE Archive) e; **49tc.** *Robert Wytt* (Barrie Wentzell / Repfoto) e; **49tr.** Cover of Pink Floyd's Album *The Wall* (EMI Records, Hayes Middlesex, England)

e; **50l.** *The Cure* (The Cure Archive) d; **50r.** *Interior of CBGB* (DoGi Archive, Florence) d; **51tc.** *A Punk* (Robert Ellis / Repfoto) d; **51tr.** *An Oil Yard* (DoGi Archive, Florence) d; **52tl.** *MTV Logo* (Music TeleVision) d; **52bl.** *Freddy Mercury* (Robert Ellis / Repfoto) d; **52c.** Poster for the Film *Flashdance* (Paramount Picture Corporation) e; **52bc.** Photo of the video clip *Thriller* by John Landis (Jackson Archive) e; **53t.** *The Fall of the Berlin Wall* (Associated Press Photo) d; **53b.** *Photo of a CD* (DoGi Archive, Florence) e; **54t.** *Pet Shop Boys* (DoGi Archive, Florence) d; **54c.** *Laurie Anderson* (Giovanni Canitano Photo) d; **55tc.** *Brian Eno* (DoGi Archive, Florence) d; **55tr.** *A Synthesizer* (Yamaha Music Media Corporation) e; **55b.** *A Drum Machine* (Yamaha Music Media Corporation) e; **56.** *R.E.M.* (Giovanni Canitano Photo) e; **57l.** *Born to Run* (Eric Meola Photo) e; **57r.** *Bob Geldof* (Farabolafoto) d; **58tl.** *Afrika Bambaataa* (Corbis / Daniel Lane) d; **58tr.** *Tupac Shakur* (Associated Press Photo) d; **59tc.** *Prince* (Giovanni Canitano Photo) d; **59tr.** *Niggers with Attitude* (Michael Johansson / Repfoto) d; **60a.** *Dead Kennedys* (DoGi Archives, Florence) d; **60c.** *Björk* (DoGi Archive); **61t.** *Sub Pop Logo* (Sub Pop Records) e; **61b.** *Peter Gabriel* (Giovanni Canitano Photo).

Cover (clockwise from top left):
1. 7; **2.** 12tr; **3.** 44; **4.** Rocker in Brighton (1964) photo by G. Roger/D.R.; **5.** 34; **6.** 10; **7.** 39; **8.** 33tr; **9.** 16; **10.** 38tr; **11.** 11; **12.** Debby Boone, photo of Pat Boone Family Group 1968 (IGDA) d; **13.** 16b; **14.** 29tr; **15.** 11tl; **16.** 12tl; **17.** Cover of *We Are the World* (© United Support of Artists for Africa) d; **18.** 45; **19.** A psychedelic concert playbill (Edizioni La Republica) d; **20.** 49tr.
Back Cover:
Andrea Ricciardi

CONTENTS

LEADERS

Rebellious music in the generation at war with its fathers—rock, from the 1950s on, forever changed the face of popular music. Rock was the preferred language of young people, and a favorite target for censors and traditionalists. It accompanied, reflected, and at times even caused events. Rock was the voice of protest in the 1960s and of disillusionment in the 1970s. Vital and energetic, the child of African-American music, rock changed form and objectives again and again, at times aspiring to become art, at other times returning to its traditional role as popular entertainment.

1. James Dean The handsome, rebellious actor became a youth idol in the 1950s.

2. John F. Kennedy (JFK) He was president of the United States from 1960 to 1963.

3. Martin Luther King, Jr. He led the movement for African-American civil rights in the 1960s.

4. Ed Sullivan He was a television host whose show featured historic appearances by Elvis Presley, the Beatles, and the Doors.

5. Alan Freed A disc jockey of the 1950s, he was the first to give the name "rock and roll" to the new combination of rhythm and blues and country music.

6. Chuck Berry and Little Richard Berry was rock's first poet; Little Richard was the showman with the primal howl.

7. Elvis Presley Though he did not invent rock and roll back in the 1950s, he was its undisputed king.

8. The Beatles They were four young men from Liverpool, England, who revolutionized popular music in the 1960s.

9. The Rolling Stones In "swinging London," the ironic, ambiguous Rolling Stones restored rock to its defiant roots.

10. BOB DYLAN
In the 1960s he showed generations of musicians that popular music could also be poetic and mature.

11. THE GRATEFUL DEAD AND THE VELVET UNDERGROUND
The first was associated with the "hippy" and psychedelic movements of the 1960s; the second was closer to the New York avant-garde scene.

12. JIMI HENDRIX
He revolutionized guitar playing in the late 1960s.

13. JANIS JOPLIN
In the 1960s she gave the most intense vocal performances in rock history.

14. THE SEX PISTOLS
The "baddest" band in the history of rock made its debut in 1976.

15. LED ZEPPELIN
The fathers of hard rock and heavy metal, they climbed to the top of the charts in the 1970s with a hard, distorted, amplified sound.

16. BRUCE SPRINGSTEEN
In the carefree, hypocritical decade of the 1980s, he raised the banner of true proletarian rock.

17. KURT COBAIN
He enriched the music of the 1990s with his energy, if only for a short time.

PEACETIME AMERICA

In the early 1950s, the United States appeared to be the free, prosperous land foretold by the longtime myth. The country's overall wealth, along with its per capita income—the average amount of money earned by each individual in a year—showed extraordinary growth. Products that were once reserved for the privileged classes, such as automobiles and electronic appliances, became available to everyone. This unprecedented wealth seemed to put an end to the traditional conflicts between the rich and the poor. "Everyone agrees about everything," asserted *Life* magazine, and everyone did seem to share the values of work, family, and order that had made that economic miracle possible.

♦ THE COLD WAR
Having become both a military and an economic superpower, the United States competed on ideological terms with what was then the Soviet Union. The United States promoted parliamentary democracy and capitalism, while the Soviet Union was the expression of a Communist political and economic system. This competition came to be known as the Cold War since there was no actual exchange of fire between armies, and in its earliest phases, it led to a strengthening of positions in both countries. In the United States, the psychosis of the "Red Menace" was fed by the campaign of Senator Joseph McCarthy (above) against intellectuals, artists, and celebrities suspected of having sympathy for the enemy. Many lost their jobs following accusations of disloyalty, and an atmosphere of blind intolerance gripped the nation.

♦ ELECTRICAL APPLIANCES
Between 1940 and 1956 the average income of the American family rose from $5,000 to nearly $7,000.

The additional $2,000 was used to purchase electrical appliances, as well as more traditional consumer goods.

THE TYPICAL AMERICAN FAMILY
In the summer of 1952 a typical American family posed in front of their home with their appliances and luxuries. The father worked for a living, the mother was a housewife, and they had two children.

♦ POPULAR SINGERS
The silky, romantic voices of Doris Day and Bing Crosby filled peaceful domestic homes throughout the country.

♦ **HAIRCUTS**
Military-style crew cuts, comfortable and practical, were worn by fathers and sons alike.

♦ **TELEVISION**
In the 1950s there were more than twenty-seven million television sets in American homes. Approximately three hundred different stations offered nearly seven hours a day of programming.

♦ **POP MUSIC**
The saccharine pop music of the times reflected the apparently calm and peaceful atmosphere of the early 1950s. Bing Crosby, Doris Day (above), and Perry Como were the most famous interpreters of this primarily melodic music, which featured smooth, limpid vocals, and to which only Frank Sinatra brought certain original touches. Divided into three subcategories—sentimental, melodramatic, and frivolous—pop music did not seek to stir up the passions of adults or young people. There were no references to physical love, and hints of forbidden love or love that was unacceptable were deliberately avoided. The pop music industry endlessly reproduced a single model that, without any real alternatives, dominated public taste, earning 90 percent of record sales.

NEW REBELS

An unexpected conflict between the generations broke out in the happy, industrious America of those years. Young rebels, "lost" and disdainful, began to criticize their parents' values and lifestyle, denouncing their hypocrisy, conformism, blind obedience, and near-religious devotion to work. It was then that young people created their own, exclusive world of passions and trends, in which rock and roll (R&R), the new musical style, played a fundamental role. Thanks in part to the extraordinary economic boom that put more money in their pockets, young people indulged their immense need for fun and escapism, which in itself subverted the traditional values of sacrifice and work.

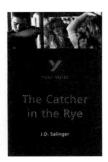

♦ THE CATCHER IN THE RYE
No modern generation, it seems, comes of age without developing a passion for *The Catcher in the Rye*, the now-classic novel by American writer J. D. Salinger, published in 1951 (above, the cover of an American edition). With the adventures of Holden Caulfield, a gifted and sensible young man incapable of "adjusting" to the rules at school, at home, and in society as a whole, Salinger created one of the prototypes for young people in the 1950s, who, almost instinctively, dared to repudiate mainstream American values and behavior. They were "maladjusted" individuals who, like Holden, challenged "duty" with laziness, and the American myth of competition and success with disinterested generosity and love for the weak.

DRIVE-IN MOVIES
Drive-in movies, an open-air theater where films were watched from the back seat of the car, sometimes in the arms of a boyfriend or girlfriend, were the new passion for young Americans in the 1950s.

TROUBLED FAMILIES
Only four years had gone by, but the atmosphere in the average American household had changed. The teenagers in high school were rebellious, and their parents no longer understood them.

♦ SUBVERSIVE MUSIC
Rock and roll became one of the secret codes of a world that belonged exclusively to young people, where adults were forbidden to enter.

♦ CRUISING
One of the favorite pastimes of young people was driving through town.

Rock and roll, playing on the car radio, was their constant companion.

♦ YOUNG PEOPLE AND ADVERTISING
Young Americans had a seemingly boundless desire for entertainment in the 1950s. This fact could not fail to attract the attention of advertising agencies and they discovered that young audiences were even more willing than adults or elderly people to spend the money at their disposal. It was at this time that most advertising came to be targeted to young people, to pander to and multiply their desires. Magazines and television began to be filled with ads that used the new, youthful styles of film and music to invite viewers to purchase fast, sporty cars, leather jackets, the jeans worn by Marlon Brando or James Dean, and "wicked" rock and roll records. Above, an ad from the 1950s.

JAMES DEAN

"REBEL WITHOUT A CAUSE"

♦ THE UNIFORM
The official uniform was the type of tight, white T-shirt James Dean wore under his leather jacket, and tight jeans at all times—not only at work.

♦ REBEL WITHOUT A CAUSE
Teen-aged boys developed a passion for James Dean, the actor who became an idol with the film *Rebel without a Cause* (1955), the archetypal story of fragile youth, misunderstood by their preoccupied parents.

ORIGINS

During the 1940s many African-Americans left the South, still a hostile and racist area, for the industrial cities of the North. They took a suitcase, their few belongings, and sometimes a guitar with them. Among them were interpreters of country blues, an African-American musical genre in which a solo voice, accompanied by acoustic guitar, shifts between the five-note African scale and the seven-note European scale. Transferred to the chaotic cities of the North, the blues absorbed their atmosphere and sounds; acoustic guitars were soon replaced by electric, amplified instruments, and rhythms became more animated. A new musical form was born, known as rhythm and blues (R&B). Combined with "white" country music—the popular music of the South— it would lead to the rock and roll revolution.

♦ RHYTHM AND BLUES
During the 1940s jazz was transformed from dance music into sophisticated art music. This led many African-American musicians to reemphasize the traditional, rhythmic aspects of their music, the blues came alive with a stronger beat, and such artists as T-Bone Walker, Muddy Waters (above), and Howlin' Wolf began to use the electric guitar in blues music. The blues soon became music for bands, with a rhythm section keeping the beat (contrabass, piano, and drums), along with solo instruments such as guitar and sax.
This same combination, which would ultimately form the basis for rock and roll, gave rise to rhythm and blues, a new type of music, with harsh vocals and more daring lyrics, in contrast to the demure texts of white popular music.

♦ SOUTHERN ROOTS
Less privileged white people were also drawn to the northern metropolises. People in the big city, however, did not change their musical tastes, and country music was soon performed on local radio stations.

♦ IMMIGRATION
Between 1940 and 1950, 214,000 African-Americans moved to Chicago from the southern United States. Most came from the Mississippi Delta area.

♦ RHYTHM
Rhythm and blues is a "physical" style of music, for listening and dancing. This was an essential characteristic of African music, and soon became a part of rock and roll.

CHICAGO IN 1952
On a cold fall morning in 1952 a bus pulled into Chicago with its usual load of newcomers—mostly African-Americans, fleeing from the intolerance of the South and hoping for a more peaceful and prosperous life.

♦ FATS DOMINO
The plump and friendly-looking Fats Domino created an upbeat, exhilarating brand of rhythm and blues. He was a favorite of young white people, too.

♦ COUNTRY
During the 1920s white music from the rural Southeast, played primarily on string instruments, came to be known as "hillbilly" music. By the 1930s, hillbilly music was already showing the influence of the blues and of the dance rhythms of African-American music. The same was true of another emerging style of country music, inspired by cowboy life, called "western" music. The genre's new name, country and western, reflected this change. By the end of the 1940s, with the exception of Hank Williams (above), country had eliminated most traces of African-American influence. Still, it was Bill Haley's western swing and Elvis Presley's hillbilly boogie—styles that had already assimilated, to some extent, the lively rhythms of African-American music, that would contribute to the birth of rock and roll.

♦ RHYTHM AND BLUES
Electric guitar and saxophone solos were some of the defining features of rhythm and blues, the new African-American musical form.

THE NEW MUSIC ARRIVES

The need for a new type of music that would unleash energies and tell about real life led a growing number of young white people to explore the more exhilarating world of African-American music. Disc jockeys (deejays) at local radio stations, the first to take note of this trend, were already promoting the driving beat of rhythm and blues by 1951. Among them, Alan Freed, a deejay at Station WJW, Cleveland, Ohio, was the first to use the term "rock and roll" to talk about rhythm and blues and about the earliest attempts to combine rhythm and blues with white country music. Within a few years, the popularity of rhythm and blues and rock and roll records began to soar in the national charts, becoming the new touchstone for a young generation at war with adults.

♦ THE JUKEBOX
Dismissed as "noise" by adults, rock and roll was at first banished from living room record players and radios, finding refuge in the recently invented transistor radios, which young people listened to almost furtively in the garage or in their own bedrooms. The jukebox, which enjoyed unprecedented growth in the 1950s following the introduction of the 45 rpm record, was another critically important haven for rock and roll.
Available wherever young people gathered, jukeboxes allowed young people to hear and dance to their new music, rock and roll, with the mere flick of a coin—at an appropriate volume, and without their parents' censorship. Above, a jukebox from the 1950s.

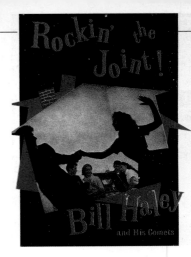

♦ BILL HALEY AND THE COMETS
Bill Haley's name is forever associated with one of rock's archetypal songs, *Rock Around the Clock*, which became, in May 1955, the first rock and roll song to reach number one on the all-important pop charts. Above, the cover of *Rockin' the Joint*.

ON THE AIR AT WINS, NEW YORK
Alan Freed was hired by WINS in 1954, after the great success with young Cleveland audiences of his broadcasts of African-American music.

♦ ALAN FREED
He promoted the new musical style in 1951, courageously airing R&B, organizing rock and roll concerts and events, and earning the trust of thousands of young people. Freed also brought about a change in deejays' style, which became livelier and more informal.

ROCK AND ROLL AND RACISM

In 1954 the Supreme Court's *Brown v. The Board of Education* decision made racial discrimination illegal in public schools.

✦ THE CHARTS

Two of Freed's colleagues look over *Billboard* magazine's charts. At the time, music was divided into different types, corresponding to different audiences: pop, country and western (favored by southern whites), and finally "race music" or R&B, targeted to an exclusively African-American public.

✦ REQUESTS

The white public's demand for records by African-American artists Chuck Berry and Little Richard showed how rock and roll was becoming associated with young people's growing antiracism.

✦ RECORD LABEL EXECUTIVES

The enormous power of such deejays as Alan Freed to influence the taste of young people led some record label executives to promote their artists' airplay by offering hefty bribes directly to the radio personalities.

✦ ASCAP VERSUS BMI

ASCAP is an association made up of artists, publishers, composers, and lyricists that also negotiated the amount of money paid to composers each time one of their records was broadcast on the radio. In 1939, after ASCAP and several radio associations failed to reach an agreement, ASCAP, which included most leading pop artists, prohibited radio stations from playing its members' music. In response, radio stations founded an alternative organization, BMI, which represented the publishers and composers of previously neglected musical styles, such as country and western and rhythm and blues. Radio stations began to play new kinds of music, including African-American music, introducing the general public to the sounds and rhythms that would later form the basis of rock and roll. Above, a vintage radio set.

✦ THE 45 RPM

Vinyl (synthetic resin) records took the place of the old 78 rpm records that were made of shellac. The new 45 rpm format was launched by RCA in 1949, and by 1955, when rock and roll was in full swing, it passed the old shellac records in sales.

INDEPENDENT LABELS

♦ CHUCK BERRY'S LYRICS
Chuck Berry (above), a guitarist and singer, stands out in the history of rock also as a lyricist. His verses were admired for two reasons: First of all, they told stories of real life in a simple and, above all, personal language, and they established a strong bond with the world of young people. Chuck Berry brought rock and roll closer to young people, not only through exciting rhythms, but also by telling about their world in a straightforward way. In "School Day" (1957) and "Sweet Little Sixteen" (1958), various aspects of teenagers' lives were described: high school, love for cars and new music, conflicts with adults, dreams of love. They were simple stories, and their protagonists could even be considered banal, but most young people were able to identify with them.

During the early 1950s the record industry was dominated by large record labels—known as "majors"—that concentrated their energies on the vast and more profitable pop market. The "indies"— smaller record labels—in contrast, survived by cultivating musical styles that had local followings. The indies soon took notice of the enthusiasm of young white audiences for rhythm and blues, and thought—correctly, as it turned out—that they could garner a much larger market share. They increased their output of rhythm and blues recordings and supported the first experiments in rock and roll, whose most successful fruits were the early recordings by Chuck Berry and Elvis Presley. By 1956 the independent labels finally made their mark, reaching the top of the national pop charts with rock and roll music.

CHESS
In the Chicago recording studios of the legendary Chess label, one of the most active independent labels, Chuck Berry rehearsed on the electric guitar.

♦ CHUCK BERRY
He was one of rock and roll's first heroes. He arrived in Chicago in 1955 and met his idol, Muddy Waters, the famous blues guitarist, who introduced him to the Chess brothers. That same year, Berry recorded his first great success, "Maybelline."

♦ HIS STYLE
Chuck Berry developed a style in which electric guitar alternated chords, providing rhythmic accompaniment with surprising solo bursts.

♦ THE CHESS BROTHERS
Leonard and Phil Chess, immigrants from Poland, founded Aristocratic Records, whose name they changed in 1950 to Chess. They recorded all the major blues artists such as Muddy Waters and Howlin' Wolf, as well as rock and roll sensation Chuck Berry.

♦ CLERKS
Clerks packed up the records, which were then sent to customers. Without a solid distribution network, the independents depended on mail orders for their greatest source of revenue.

♦ MAJORS
Surprised by the extraordinary success of R&B records with young white people, the major labels reacted by creating "covers," picking out a handsome young white man, who was nonthreatening in appearance and had a sweet, pleasant voice. They had a successful rhythm and blues cut rerecorded, sugar-coating its rhythms, added a pop orchestration, and changed the words, removing all references to sex. The king of covers was Pat Boone (above), a quiet, clean-cut young man who always managed to top the national charts with newly arranged versions of rock and blues cuts, even though the originals were invariably more interesting. His version of Little Richard's "Tutti Frutti" overtook the original in the charts.

♦ DRUMS
Drums grounded the rhythm section and, with the piano and the electric guitar, formed the basis of the distinctive Chess sound.

ELVIS: THE KING

In 1954 rock and roll found its king. He came from Memphis, was nineteen years old, and loved African-American music with a passion. His name was Elvis Presley. That year he entered the studios of the Sun label to cut his first record, and a new sound was born: rock and roll with heavy country accents. Local radio stations began playing the record, and it created a sensation. Elvis then embarked on his first tour in the South, making his entrance on stage in loud, gaudy clothes. He brandished his guitar like a weapon, playing it with an unprecedented energy, even breaking its strings. He swayed his pelvis, gyrating in a free and sensual way, he rolled on the ground, and crawled around on all fours. He excited and delighted young people, who found in him and his music the perfect combination of rebellion and entertainment.

✦ SUN'S EARLY YEARS

In 1952 a former sound technician, Sam Phillips, founded the Sun label in Memphis, Tennessee, and began recording southern blues musicians. With the explosion of rhythm and blues, Phillips felt that if he could "find a white man who sings like a black man [he] could make a million." Elvis Presley arrived in 1954. Phillips called him in for some rehearsals with Bill Black (bass) and Scotty Moore (guitar). Elvis played a few country ballads, but did not make a great impression. Casually, he began to improvise variations on a blues song, and then came the miracle: the driving rhythm of the bass and the guitar accompanying Elvis's light but passionate voice, a completely original style, a synthesis of African-American rhythms and country vocals known as "rockabilly," one of the great achievements of rock and roll. Above, Sun's logo.

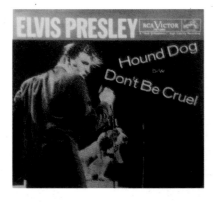

✦ TOPPING THE CHARTS

In 1956 Elvis reached number one in pop, country, and R&B charts with "Don't Be Cruel" and "Hound Dog." Rock and roll and its heroes were breaking down the traditional divisions of taste among white and African-American audiences.

✦ THE PELVIS

The impact of Elvis's pelvis mimicking sexual movements was so shocking that Ed Sullivan demanded that Elvis be shown from only the waist up on his popular television show.

✦ ELVIS'S FILMS

Elvis always dreamed of becoming a Hollywood movie star, and succeeded thanks to an interminable series of somewhat boring comedies that were designed primarily to promote his music and his image.

✦ CLOTHES

Elvis's stage costumes were brightly colored, in the style of African-American and country artists.

♦ **SIDEBURNS**
In 1950s America, it was truck drivers, for the most part, who wore sideburns. Elvis copied their virility and spontaneity.

♦ **FORELOCK**
Elvis loved wearing a forelock, a style he had copied from actor Tony Curtis.

♦ **THE LOOK**
The twenty-year-old Elvis Presley wore an arrogant smirk at times, and at other times, an expression of innocence. His youthful, almost feminine looks, combined with his masculine sideburns, gave him an androgynous look.

♦ **HIS RCA CONTRACT**
In 1955 Elvis appeared on the national country charts and showed he was more than just a promising talent. A Dutch immigrant, Colonel Tom Parker (above), became his exclusive manager and had him immediately sign a contract with RCA, a major label, which took Elvis on for the then-astronomical figure of $40,000. Joining RCA changed Elvis's style; his vocals grew cooler, and his accompaniments began to include drums and electric guitar. It was still rock and roll, but the energy that had come from the spontaneity of his early performances began to diminish. Elvis's talent, however, was immense, as was the power of rock and roll. A number of television appearances (on Ed Sullivan's show, for instance), and the nationwide release of his records won him unprecedented popularity.

♦ **BONFIRES FOR ELVIS**
Elvis's great success and his gyrating pelvis inspired an almost frenzied hostility among conservative religious groups, who burned his records in public bonfires.

THE HOWL

Driving rhythms, electric and amplified sounds, "scandalous" interpretations—these traits had come to characterize rock and roll when an eccentric young African-American man, Little Richard, added a raw, daring vocal style, a combination of singing and shouting. Little Richard's contributions unleashed indignation and fear among industry experts and traditionalists. The former rejected a musical style that made it a point of pride to demonstrate a lack of technical polish, a mixture of harmony and noise, and the combination of singing and shouting. The latter were terrified by a type of music that represented an assault on good manners, self-control, and proper behavior.

♦ THE KILLER
When Elvis left Sun, Sam Phillips acquired a small sum of money, enough to balance Sun's books and to attempt to break into the national market. Such ambitious plans, however, required new talent. In 1956 Jerry Lee Lewis (above), whose nickname was "The Killer," arrived from Louisiana. Influenced by gospel, the sacred music of African-Americans, and by country music, he created an energetic brand of rockabilly, characterized by exciting piano playing. In 1956 he broke onto the charts for the first time with "Crazy Arms," and exploded the following year with "Whole Lotta Shakin' Goin' On." His concerts were also memorable: Lewis, with a demonic air, pounded on his piano and pushed it around the stage, much to the delight of his fans.

♦ RELIGIOUS SHOUTERS
In their vocalism and frenzied performance style, many rock and rollers were influenced by the "shouting" of preachers, who sought to commune with God through their explosive, uninhibited performances.

LITTLE RICHARD
He was born in Macon, Georgia, in 1932. As a child, he sang in his city's Baptist choir, then went on the road as a soloist. In 1955 he made his debut recording, "Tutti Frutti," his first big success.

♦ THE PIANO
In rock, the piano does not play its traditional role of "leading" the melody, but instead provides rhythmic accompaniment through driving, repetitive chords—three or more notes played at the same time.

♦ CARL LEE PERKINS
The Sun label's new star, Perkins topped the pop, country, and rhythm and blues charts in 1956 with his famous "Blue Suede Shoes" (also made popular by Elvis Presley).

♦ MAKEUP
Little Richard's unprecedented use of makeup and explicit references to homosexuality reinforced the new image of rock and roll. His impact, however, was relatively limited, since African-American artists were not expected to show the respectability that was demanded of white artists.

♦ HOWLING
Little Richard's raw shouts in "Tutti Frutti" undermined the vocal sound of American pop music, which had required a trained voice, pure intonation, high notes, and clear diction.

♦ POSTURE
Little Richard, with his controversial way of "abusing" the piano, showed that rock piano was very different from the idealized classical instrument.

PRIVATE PRESLEY

The formidable success of Elvis Presley, Chuck Berry, and Little Richard persuaded the major record companies to invest in rock and roll, but in their hands, the new musical style and its leaders were transformed; the music became much softer and more sentimental, and the musicians were transformed into well-behaved, harmless boys. American society, in the meantime, bore down on the rebels. Chuck Berry was denounced for an alleged sexual relationship with a minor girl, Alan Freed found himself embroiled in the "payola" scandal (see page 21); and Jerry Lee Lewis was publicly criticized for marrying his fourteen-year-old cousin. When Elvis, on the advice of his manager, Colonel Parker, decided to enroll in the army like a true American patriot, the once rebellious spirit of rock and roll seemed forever dead and buried.

♦ AMERICAN BANDSTAND
This was a popular television show that promoted so-called "respectable" rock and roll. Its host, Dick Clark, always appeared in a jacket and tie and demanded that his guests do the same, prohibiting any air of rebellion.

♦ BUDDY HOLLY
With his shy, innocent air and schoolboy glasses, Buddy Holly (above) certainly did not look like a rebel. However, there came a moment in his brief, glorious career when it seemed that he would be the new king of rock and roll.
In 1955 this guitarist with a passion for rhythm and blues was hired with his group to accompany the rising star Elvis Presley to Lubbock, Texas. Buddy was captivated and immediately decided to take up rock and roll. He founded the Crickets in 1957 and began recording rockabilly songs that re-created, though in a completely personal way, the sound and spirit of a young Elvis Presley. Among his great successes were "That'll Be the Day" and "Peggy Sue." In 1959 Holly's life ended tragically, in a plane crash.

♦ THE TWIST
As the decade drew to a close there was an explosion of new dances influenced by rock and roll, among them the Twist. They were strictly individual dances— not for couples—and freed from any rigid conventional dance steps.

THE END OF A MYTH
By donning his military uniform, Elvis, the symbol of youthful defiance, devastated many of his fans, while at the same time, winning the admiration of the mainstream public, as his manager had predicted. From then on, Elvis was no longer the king of rock, the music of rebellion, but the new star of pop music.

♦ **PRIVATE PRESLEY**
At the American military base in Bremerhaven, West Germany, Private Presley answered the call of patriotic duty.

♦ **A TRAGIC NIGHT**
The night of February 3, 1959, Buddy Holly was killed in an Iowa plane crash, along with the popular new star Ritchie Valens, who wrote "La Bamba," and other tour members. At left, the crash site.

♦ **THE PAYOLA SCANDAL**
"Payola," in professional jargon, means a bribe or a cut. It became almost certain that deejays were paid off to promote certain records. This led to a 1960 congressional investigation that sought not only to stamp out corrupt elements in the record industry, but also to punish the various parties—BMI, independent record labels, and deejays—that had promoted rock and roll and threatened the monopoly by majors and ASCAP. One famous victim of this campaign was controversial deejay Alan Freed (above), who was instantly fired by his radio station after being accused of accepting $30,000 from six different record labels.
Freed was probably taking the heat for his strong support of African-American music and his bitter criticism of the "cover" phenomenon. Hounded by the IRS for income tax evasion, he eventually died of cirrhosis of the liver.

♦ **THE COLONEL**
It was in Germany that Elvis met his future wife, Priscilla Beaulieu, then fourteen years old, the daughter of an American colonel.

♦ **AMERICAN BASES**
In an attempt to halt a possible expansion into Europe by the Soviet Union, the United States, with the support of its allies, built its own formidable military bases overseas, most notably in West Germany.

MY NAME IS BOB DYLAN

♦ **WOODY GUTHRIE**
Woody Guthrie (above) was the hero of the new folk music, from the American South that combined traditional northern European ballads with lyrics conveying social protest. Guthrie was born to a poor Oklahoma family in 1912. He left home at sixteen and wandered throughout the South doing odd jobs. A year later, he learned to play the guitar and began to perform in the street, where he sang of the suffering of underprivileged people, denouncing the exploitation of the poor, describing an America that was very different from its official image. After working at a Los Angeles radio station and enrolling in the army, he returned to New York and settled in Greenwich Village, the neighborhood of counterculture artists and intellectuals, where he composed his most famous songs, "This Land Is Your Land" and "Tom Joad."

The glossy, innocent rock and roll promoted by the major labels influenced many young Americans, mostly students, to investigate musical styles that were less commercially compromised. As a result, the folk tradition enjoyed a revival in the early 1960s— music "for the people" that told stories of poor people and those who lived on the edge. The undisputed leader of this folk revival was Bob Dylan, a young man from the Midwest with a harsh, nasal voice, who expressed a powerful combination of poetic language and social criticism. Dylan, throughout an extraordinarily creative career that saw him fuse folk with rock, demonstrated that popular music could take on political themes using a newly sophisticated language.

WASHINGTON SQUARE
Dylan went to New York in 1961 and immediately moved to bohemian Greenwich Village, performing in coffeehouses, where folk music was popular and greatly appreciated, and also playing for his own enjoyment with his friends in Washington Square.

♦ **THE AUDIENCE**
Artists and intellectuals made up the audiences of Dylan and Guthrie, for the most part, people who were on the edges of mainstream culture and critical of American society and its values of money and success.

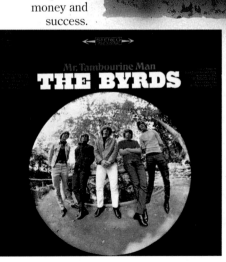

♦ **THE BYRDS**
They were the first folk-rock group to become popular. In 1965 their electric version of Bob Dylan's "Tambourine Man" reached the top of the national charts.

Dylan's lyrics

Throughout Bob Dylan's career, he tended to alternate fierce, lucid social protests, written in extremely poetic language, vivid descriptions of reality, and a highly personal exploration of the self.

♦ Bob Dylan

He was born Robert Zimmerman to a middle-class Minnesota family in 1941. Thunderstruck by Elvis Presley as a young man, he developed a passion for folk music and for Woody Guthrie in particular. He is said to have taken his stage name from the Irish poet Dylan Thomas, whose works he greatly admired.

♦ Greenwich Village

Artists and intellectuals flocked to this New York neighborhood reminiscent of old European cities with its low buildings, intimate nightclubs, and little shops.

♦ Folk rock

Already a celebrated folk singer, Bob Dylan marked a turning point in his own artistic evolution and in the history of rock by fusing his own poetic lyrics, the folk sound of the harmonica, and ballad structures with the amplified sound of the electric guitar and a rhythm section typical of rock and roll (drums and bass). This combination came to be known as folk rock. Dylan's evolution was not welcomed by folk lovers; at the 1965 Newport folk festival, the public booed Dylan with his leather jacket and electric guitar. With his folk-rock songs, Dylan managed to reach out to a wider public without compromising his art and, above all, to bring a newly sophisticated language to rock. His example would inspire many future rock artists. Above, Bob Dylan.

THE FAB FOUR

In the early 1960s a new and totally unexpected revolution in pop music came from England—the Beatles, a musical group made up of four young men from the poor neighborhoods of Liverpool, who had grown up listening to Chuck Berry and Elvis Presley. Handsome, full of life, and engaging, they created a totally new style of music, built on chords that no one had dreamed of using earlier, and on strong, driving rhythms. Throughout the western world, young people identified with their music, and the Beatles became role models and trendsetters to a degree not even Elvis Presley had been able to match.

♦ **PAUL McCartney**
With John Lennon, he made up the most celebrated team of songwriters in the history of rock. He had a great talent for melodic, up-tempo songs.

♦ **THEIR BEGINNINGS**
The Beatles began performing in 1960, in rather disreputable Hamburg clubs where the audiences were made up primarily of drunken sailors. With their leather jackets and long hair, they played a loud, howling style of rock, attracting the attention of an indifferent public. They also played at the Cavern Club in Liverpool, where they built up a loyal local following. In 1962, thanks in part to their manager Brian Epstein, who had changed their image, the Beatles began recording for EMI-Parlophone with producer George Martin. Their first single, "Love Me Do," reached number seventeen in the charts. In 1964, after a tumultuously received appearance on Ed Sullivan's television show, their popularity soared and they hit number one with their second single, "Please Please Me," the title track of their first, extremely successful LP (above).

♦ **HAIRSTYLES**
The Beatles' hairstyles, slightly longer than was traditional for men at that time, became a symbol of freedom and were soon copied by young people everywhere.

♦ **BRIAN EPSTEIN**
He became the Beatles' manager after hearing them at the Cavern in 1961. He immediately changed the group's image, and was largely instrumental in making them an international sensation. He died in 1967.

♦ **SAILORS**
Young people in Liverpool learned about the latest musical trends in the United States from American sailors passing through the port.

THE CAVERN
In 1962 the Beatles performed at the Cavern, Liverpool's celebrated nightclub that had been dug out of the cellars of the British railroad. They got their start here before finding worldwide fame.

THE BEATLES'
Yeah...Yeah...Yeah
CANDY
50 SUGAR DELIGHTS
25 INDIVIDUAL COLLECTOR
BOXES ... WITH COLORFUL
BEATLE CHARACTERS ...
FREE HAND-PUPPET INSIDE!

♦ **ROCK AND BUSINESS**
Colonel Tom Parker, Elvis Presley's manager, was the first to use a rock star's image to promote commercial products. Brian Epstein followed his example with the Beatles.

♦ **RINGO STARR**
Ringo joined the Beatles as a drummer in 1962. He provided the rhythmic background for the group, and disliked drum solos.

♦ **JOHN LENNON AND GEORGE HARRISON**
Balking at the traditional sounds of rock chords and rhythms, John, on rhythmic guitar, was the strongest personality in the group. George, on solo guitar, was a gifted instrumentalist.

♦ **THE BRITISH INVASION**
The advent of the Beatles era was important because it showed that rock and roll could survive and even flourish outside of American borders. It began in 1964 with the Beatles' first U.S. tour, when a sharply focused publicity campaign masterminded by Epstein and, above all, the group's stunning performance on *The Ed Sullivan Show* created unprecedented excitement. The "Fab Four" immediately rose to the top of the charts, staying there for weeks at a time. Having demolished the taboo that American music could be exported to England but not the reverse, they showed that there was room on the American market for the entire range of English "beat" music, which included Gerry and the Pacemakers (above), the Kinks, the Searchers, and the Rolling Stones.

SWINGING LONDON

The Beatles' music, Mary Quant's styles, and David Bailey's photographs made London of the 1960s one of the most stimulating and captivating places in the world, the global capital of an avant-garde cultural movement that redefined the very way art and fashion were conceived. In the course of that frenetic decade, English designers promoted the idea that everyday items—from can openers to washing machines—had to be not only functional, but also beautiful in form. At the same time, young artists asserted that popular forms, including comic strips, advertisements, graphic design, science fiction, and B-movies, could become or deserved to be considered true art.

♦ THE BABY BOOM
After World War II Britain did not enjoy the exceptional economic growth of the United States. It was only in 1954, in fact, that food rationing was suspended, while the demographic explosion of the 1940s, similar to that in the United States, created in the less wealthy Britain of the 1960s the problem of youth unemployment. However, the country was substantially more prosperous in the 1960s, and the strong welfare state, providing free basic services, managed, to some extent, to solve the problems related to unemployment. Within this context, the disposable income available to young Britons began to grow, but not to the same degree as for their American peers. A decade later, they too built their own world of trends and customs. Above, a London suburb.

A PHOTOGRAPHER'S STUDIO
Many of the defining images of the "swinging" London of the 1960s came from the studio of the talented young photographer David Bailey.

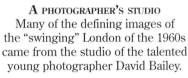

♦ BEATLEMANIA
The Beatles phenomenon burst on the scene in 1963. The group was constantly hounded by the media and the fans, and their appearances caused hysterical scenes everywhere, especially where their female fans gathered. With the Beatles, rock music became the primary expression of the tastes and aspirations of youth culture, even eclipsing the movies.

♦ CARNABY STREET
New fashions were born on this London street: English designers understood that young people needed an outfit that would not only look good but would make a lifestyle statement, or evoke a specific world and image. Thus, young people became interested in the most varied accessories: pins, buckles, and so on.

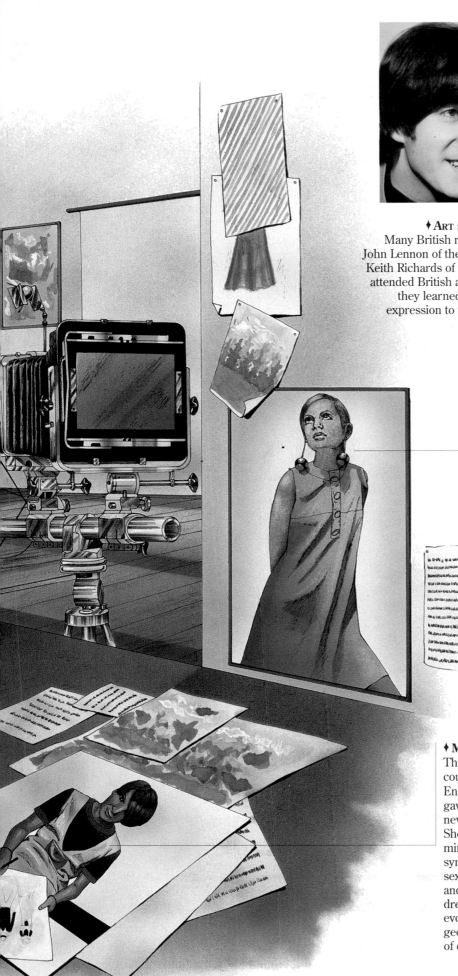

♦ ART SCHOOL
Many British rock stars, from John Lennon of the Beatles (above) to Keith Richards of the Rolling Stones, attended British art schools, where they learned to give free expression to their creativity.

♦ DESIGN
In the 1960s British design attracted worldwide attention. Both specialized journals and popular weeklies began carrying photos of Mary Quant's fashions, of Leyland automobiles, and of Kinner and Calvert's advertisements. Their common denominator was based on rigid, geometric forms. Above, a typical design object of 1960s England, the 1961 Morris Mini Cooper automobile.

♦ TWIGGY
Thin as a rail, she was the fashion model who exemplified swinging London, with her Mary Quant dresses and her famous short haircut, created by Vidal Sassoon.

♦ OPTICAL ART
"Op Art" featured identical geometric forms but highly contrasting colors, repeating them in series so as to create optical effects. Above, a 1963 work by Victor de Vasarely, the Hungarian-born French painter.

♦ MARY QUANT
This young, courageous English designer gave fashion a new direction. She invented the miniskirt, the symbol of the sexual revolution, and designed dresses that evoked the geometric forms of optical art.

THE NEW BAD BOYS

In Beatles-mad London a new English group emerged, the Rolling Stones, who brought rock back to the rude, rebellious spirit that had characterized its beginnings. Their leaders were Mick Jagger, an exuberant vocal soloist who assumed provocative, sensual poses, and Keith Richards, a talented guitarist. Returning to the origins of rock and roll—to Muddy Waters and Howlin' Wolf's electronic blues—the Rolling Stones created a hard, highly amplified sound, based on the simple, effective rhythm of the electric guitar and bass.

♦ **MICK JAGGER**
A sometimes petulant voice, messy hair, and an overwhelming stage presence: Jagger brought a certain sexuality to his performances, combining masculine attitudes with an inclination toward transvestitism.

♦ **THEIR BEGINNINGS**
Mick Jagger was in love with Chicago's electronic blues, while Keith Richards had a weakness for Chuck Berry. Mick and Keith met by chance in 1960 and began to discuss their common musical passions. They founded a musical group that three years later would come to be known as the Rolling Stones. In 1963 they recorded their first single, a cover of a song by Muddy Waters. The Stones presented themselves as the defenders of pure rhythm and blues, far removed from the pop experimentation of the Beatles. That same year their manager, Loog Oldham, decided to create an aggressive image to go along with the hard blues sound of the band: long hair, jeans, rebellious attitudes. His instinct was right on the mark, and by 1964 the Stones had already reached the top of the national charts. Above, the cover for the Rolling Stones album *Around and Around.*

AN EXCITING CONCERT
In 1966 the members of the Rolling Stones were Mick Jagger (vocal solos), Keith Richards (rhythmic guitar), Brian Jones (solo guitar), Bill Wyman (bass), and Charlie Watts (drums).

♦ **FASHIONS**
The Stones' clothing symbolized their nonconformity and desire to rebel. The Rolling Stones contrasted greatly with the Beatles and the near-unanimous approval that surrounded them.

♦ **THE ARREST OF JAGGER AND RICHARDS**
On February 12, 1967, Keith Richards and Mick Jagger were arrested and put in jail for drug possession. They were in jail only a short time, but long enough for their image of "cursed" rebels to gain new emphasis.

♦ KEITH RICHARDS
The Rolling Stones' characteristic sound is based on the rhythm established by Keith Richards' guitar, which dominates the drums, the other element of the rhythm section.

♦ MODS
The young English of the 1960s, with their short hair, elegant clothing, Italian scooters, and love for jazz or The Who were known as "mods," or modernists. They rejected tradition, even the tradition of rock upheld by rockers, the opposing camp, and occasionally came to blows with them.

♦ THE WHO
A third group emerged amid the supposed antagonism between the Beatles and the Rolling Stones: The Who (above), who also aspired to be known as "bad" and "rebellious." The group's unchallenged leader was the charismatic Pete Townshend. One of the group members was Roger Daltrey, who took over the lead vocal duties. Their beginnings were similar to those of many bands of the time: rhythm and blues and a look inspired by the Rolling Stones. Then came the fateful meeting with their future manager, Peter Meaden. The Who recast their image and became a "mod" group, in appearance and in the substance of their music. Townshend, who had, in the meantime, given up blues covers to compose his own songs, was perfectly attuned to "mod" youth. He understood their rage and often smashed his guitar apart on stage.

♦ THE AUDIENCE
The Rolling Stones' harsh music and aggressive rebelliousness excited and stimulated their audiences. Actual riots occasionally broke out at their concerts.

♦ A CLOCKWORK ORANGE
This 1962 novel by Anthony Burgess tells of a gang of incomprehensibly violent young people, whom the police and the law attempt to keep in check by using troubling measures.

MARCHING FORWARD

The Kennedy administration inaugurated the 1960s and defined a New Frontier of greater liberty and social justice. It was a decade of political involvement and great hopes on the part of young people in the United States. It saw the birth of the student and peace movements, and of the nonviolent struggles for African-American civil rights, led by Reverend Martin Luther King, Jr. His hope was for the African-American community to be integrated into mainstream American society as equals. He led the crusade for equal rights and, above all, equal opportunities in education and the workplace. To this end, he organized peaceful marches and acts of civil disobedience that forced the ruling class in the United States to seek massive social reform programs.

♦ THE MOTOWN SOUND
The importance of the Detroit record label Motown in the 1960s was not limited to music alone. Motown was, in fact, the first African-American label to record and distribute music by African-American artists. Founded by Berry Gordy, a young songwriter, Motown came to symbolize the ideal of integration being promoted at the time by Martin Luther King, Jr. Along with his formidable team, Gordy created a sound that combined the energy and dance beats typical of African-American music with the techniques and easy melodic charm of white music. The result was a captivating brand of pop music—considered rather insipid by some—that, for the first time since Elvis Presley and Little Richard, won over both African-Americans and whites. Above, a poster for a concert by the Supremes (1965).

♦ A WHITE STUDENT
Martin Luther King, Jr.'s campaign for civil rights had many impassioned allies among young white people, who struggled in their high schools and on college campuses to overcome racial prejudices.

♦ ARETHA FRANKLIN
The daughter of a Detroit minister, Aretha became the queen of soul in the late 1960s, after an indifferent early career, also winning over the white public.

♦ BOB DYLAN
Folk star Bob Dylan also took part in King's march for civil rights. He exemplified a musical style whose ambition was not to entertain but to have a direct impact on American social life.

THE MARCH ON WASHINGTON
On August 28, 1963, 300,000 people, led by Martin Luther King, Jr., marched peacefully in support of equal rights for African-Americans and whites.

♦ JOHN FITZGERALD KENNEDY
A Catholic and a Democratic senator, he defeated Republican candidate Richard Nixon in 1960 and became president of the United States. His presidency, brought to a dramatic end by his 1963 assassination in Dallas, seemed to inaugurate a new era of progress in the country.

♦ THE CROWDS
The day of the march, 300,000 people gathered at the foot of the Lincoln Memorial to listen to the memorable words of Dr. King: "I have a dream that one day on the red hills of Georgia the sons of former slaves and the sons of former slave owners will be able to sit down together at the table of brotherhood."

♦ MARTIN LUTHER KING, JR.
Inspired by Gandhi's non-violent principles, King organized peaceful demonstrations during the 1960s, particularly in southern states, protesting racial discrimination against African-Americans. In 1964 he was awarded the Nobel Peace Prize. He was assassinated in 1968.

♦ SOUL
If Motown was the music of integration, soul was the music of African-American pride, conscious of and exulting in African-American diversity. Soul made few concessions to white taste; indeed, it tended to emphasize the "unseemly" aspects of African-American music: rough vocals, screams, tense rhythms, and lascivious performance styles. From a purely musical point of view, soul represented a fusion of vocal styles from gospel (African-American religious music) and the beat of rhythm and blues, punctuated frequently, especially in funk, by brass (trumpets and sax). Among the greatest interpreters of soul music was Otis Redding (above), the first to try to bring together the worlds of soul and rock, and the exhilarating, irrepressible James Brown.

THE SUMMER OF LOVE

The uneasiness and feelings of dissatisfaction that, a decade earlier, had provoked rebellious attitudes in young people, in the optimistic 1960s awoke in them a desire to build an alternative society, founded on the values of love, spirituality, and communal ownership of goods. This idea was born and developed in California, and came to be associated with the psychedelic movement, which suggested that it was possible to acquire a deeper knowledge of the self through the use of drugs. Rock became one of the primary means of communicating this point of view; California bands created "acid rock," intended, among other things, to accompany the taking of hallucinogenic substances. These same bands resisted the mainstream recording industry's systems and methods because they felt the business was too corrupted by money.

♦ THE HIPPIE MOVEMENT
As early as the end of the 1950s groups of intellectuals gathered in peaceful San Francisco, to undertake a radical critique of the most widely shared values in American society, choosing to isolate themselves and to embark on a new lifestyle. Thanks to them, by the early 1960s nonconformist ideas and lifestyles had begun to spread, which attracted mostly upper-middle-class young people: sexual freedom, concern for the environment, Asian philoso-phies as more authentic spiritual values, and drug use. The hippie movement exploded in 1965, becoming what writer Allen Ginsberg called "flower power." Such slogans as "Make love, not war" were adopted by millions of young people wearing bell-bottoms, brightly colored T-shirts, and long hair. Above, a hippie.

ACID TEST
In 1966 at San Francisco's Fillmore Theater, an acid test took place—that is, a public experiment with the hallucinogenic drug LSD's effects on creativity and the ways of perceiving reality. Music by the Grateful Dead accompanied the event.

♦ IMPROVISATION
One of the innovations of acid rock was live improvisation, along with the tendency, fueled by drug use, to stretch out songs *ad infinitum*. These were often instrumental pieces.

♦ SCREENS
Among other things, acid tests called for large screens upon which slides "corrected" with the liquid colors of psychedelia were projected, so as to make the experience all the more evocative and absorbing.

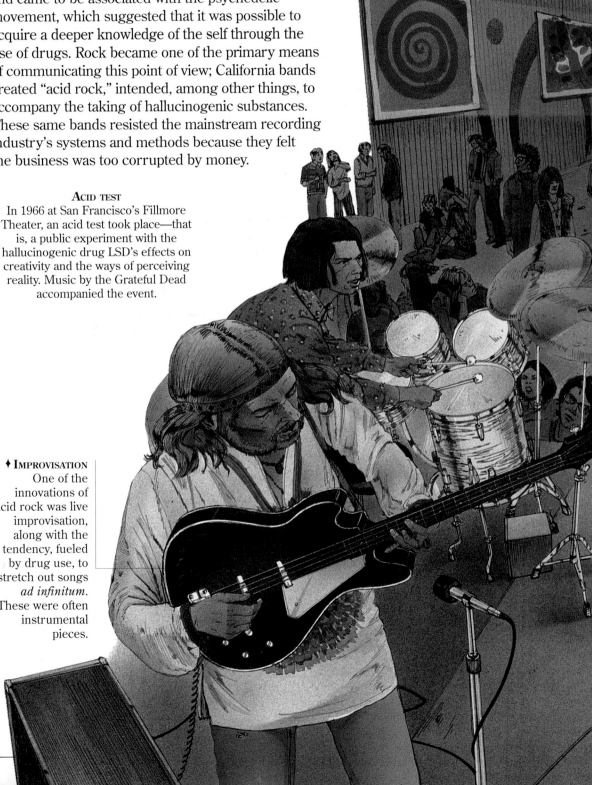

♦ THE GRATEFUL DEAD

Led by guitarist Jerry Garcia, they were the leading group of the California acid rock scene. Faithful to hippie ideals, they lived communally in the Haight-Ashbury district of San Francisco and became almost a cult with many loyal fans.

♦ AMPLIFICATION

The Grateful Dead took to playing their instruments very close to their amplifiers, causing the strings of the electric guitar to resonate with feedback, which produced a characteristic piercing sound.

♦ THE BEACH BOYS

In the early 1960s a new type of music emerged in California—surf music— and a new group, the Beach Boys. Underlying their apparently lighthearted themes—beaches, pretty girls, having fun—was music of great vocal complexity and elaboration that challenged the best work of the Beatles.

♦ PSYCHEDELIC GRAPHICS

The hippie and psychedelic scenes also inspired new, alternative forms of art. Many artists, including Wes Wilson and Rick Griffin, began designing posters, concert playbills, and album covers using the twisted forms and liquid colors characteristic of psychedelia. Above, a playbill for a psychedelic concert.

♦ KEN KESEY

A controversial writer, author of the well-known *One Flew Over the Cuckoo's Nest* (1962), he invented the acid test.

♦ ACID ROCK

Folk rock formed the basis for acid rock, an electrified version of traditional popular music, reinforced by amplification and by the frequent use of feedback, and recast in innovative forms through the use of Indian rhythms and melodic scales. Above, a poster for a concert by the Jefferson Airplane.

A HISTORIC ALBUM

For the second time in only a few years, the Beatles transformed popular music. Weary of concerts packed with screaming girls, the Beatles focused their talents on unprecedented musical explorations. These explorations took place in the recording studio, which was constantly being enhanced with new technologies. With albums like *Revolver* (1966) and, most of all, the historic *Sgt. Pepper's Lonely Hearts Club Band* (1967), the Beatles created revolutionary musical worlds, astonishing for their creative freedom and matchless ability to fuse classical music with the distortions of an electric guitar, musicals with rock and roll, background noises with Indian music.

♦ THE ALBUM
Preceded by the release of the historic single "Strawberry Fields Forever / Penny Lane" (above, cover), *Sgt. Pepper* was the fruit of more than 400 hours of painstaking work in the recording studio—at a then-unprecedented cost to EMI of £10,000. The Beatles entered the studio at the end of 1966 and emerged with the album in March of 1967, convinced they had given birth to something absolutely new. The idea of a "concept album," where the songs are related thematically, was new, and the songs themselves were innovative: "A Day in the Life," in particular, was a jewel born of the fusion of two songs, one by John Lennon, the other by Paul McCartney, both characterized by utterly different musical tones and colors and crowned with a monumental string crescendo.

♦ THE LP
In 1967 the LP outsold the single for the first time, indicating that listeners were increasingly interested in an artist's overall musical project rather than in isolated hit songs.

♦ THE SITAR
Fascinated by Indian philosophy, George Harrison also came to love Indian music. In one of his cuts on the album, "Within You Without You," Harrison played the sitar, a traditional stringed Indian instrument.

♦ GEORGE MARTIN
The Beatles owed much to their producer and arranger, George Martin, who knew how to handle their sometimes bizarre requests. One day, John Lennon asked Martin to give his songs the sound of an orange.

♦ A GROUP OF SOLOISTS
Though they were still known as a group, the Beatles were focusing increasingly on their solo work: Lennon and McCartney had stopped composing together sometime earlier, and Harrison had written some remarkable songs of his own.

THE RECORDING STUDIO
The four boys from Liverpool gathered in EMI's Studio 2 on Abbey Road during a break in the recording of *Sgt. Pepper*.

♦ STRINGS
For "A Day in the Life," the Beatles hired forty orchestra musicians. Their use of string instruments and of brass, usually limited to classical music, revealed their desire to transcend the traditional forms of rock music.

♦ THE ALBUM COVER
The year that *Sgt. Pepper* came out, psychedelia was winning many converts in England, too, not least of them the Beatles. John Lennon used LSD in the widely shared belief that it would help him acquire a better understanding of himself. His song "Lucy in the Sky with Diamonds" contains, in the view of some critics, a hidden reference to LSD in the initials of the title words. George Harrison practiced meditation, and even Paul McCartney showed a certain interest in psychedelic culture. The four Beatles made their affinities for the psychedelic movement explicit not only in their lyrics, but also by appearing on the album cover (created by pop artist Peter Blake) in unmistakably psychedelic-colored suits. Above, the cover of *Sgt. Pepper*.

♦ MIXERS
EMI made use of two new technologies in recording the album: the varispeed, which varied the tempo of a song on tape, and the dumper, used for toning down sound.

♦ THE APPROACHING BREAKUP
The Beatles went through a crisis in 1969. John Lennon, now married to Japanese artist Yoko Ono, was increasingly absorbed by his solo musical career; and he and McCartney fought over the choice of a new manager. A breakup was inevitable. Above, Lennon and Yoko Ono.

ROCK IN THE GALLERIES

Lively and instinctive, rock always seemed to be an entertaining but innocuous expression of youthful taste. With New York's Velvet Underground, however, rock became increasingly ambitious. Their lyrics, by singer and guitarist Lou Reed, inspired by "beat" writers, spoke without shame or hypocrisy of dark, forbidden realities. Their performances in the multimedia (theater, music, art) spectacles mounted by Andy Warhol put rock in intimate contact for the first time with avant-garde artists. The Velvet Underground's sound, too—essential, built on a handful of chords with typical electric guitar distortions—reflected European avant-garde musical experiments.

♦ **LOU REED'S LYRICS**
Lou Reed's lyrics have had an enormous influence on subsequent generations of rock musicians. They never attracted widespread public attention because the Velvet Underground never truly reached a vast public as Dylan or the Beatles did. Still, they became an important model for many artists in the 1970s who felt empowered to speak a different language and convey different realities. Reed had the courage and talent to use his songs to tell stories about prostitutes, transvestites, drug dealers, sadomasochism, the desolation of big cities, and drugs. And he did so mingling frank, vulgar expressions with refined poetry, and realistic episodes with images of tremendous creative power.

♦ **THEIR FIRST ALBUM**
The Velvet Underground's first album, *The Velvet Underground & Nico* (1967), was a commercial failure. Its strange cover was designed by Andy Warhol, who was their manager and directed the group in some shows.

AT THE FACTORY
The Velvet Underground attended a projection of the film made by Andy Warhol during one of their performances at the Dom. Starting in 1966 the Velvet Underground provided musical accompaniments for the multimedia (painting, poetry, dance) spectacles organized by the famous New York artist.

♦ **NICO**
A model from Berlin, unquestionably beautiful, with a somewhat dubious acting career behind her, Nico became Andy Warhol's protégée. When he began managing the Velvet Underground, he made her a vocalist in the group.

✦ THE BEAT GENERATION
From Kerouac (left) to Burroughs, the beat writers told of "different" heroes who drank, used drugs, and lived turbulent but possibly truer and more authentic lives.

✦ ANDY WARHOL
A leader of the pop art movement, Warhol appropriated and manipulated images from ads, comic strips, and films, and commonplace items (a Campbell soup can). Warhol took note of the Velvet Underground at the Bizarre Café, and decided to introduce them to the world of alternative artists and intellectuals who frequented the Factory.

✦ FRANK ZAPPA
A bizarre and versatile artist, he grew up in 1960s Los Angeles, studying music, film, video, theater, and art. Inspired by his incredibly diverse experience in avant-garde classical music, rock and roll, experimental theater, and comic strips, Frank Zappa, along with his group, the Mothers of Invention, loved to thwart expectations, mixing different genres, sounds, and languages. A great actor, capable of undertaking mad, poetic theatrical performances during his concerts, Zappa poked fun at the world of rock and its heroes who claimed they wanted to change the world in the years between psychedelia and the hippy movement, especially with the memorable title of one of his albums, *We're Only in It for the Money.*

✦ ANDY WARHOL'S CINEMA
Warhol also created experimental films. He sometimes mounted a camera in a certain spot for hours at a time and allowed it to film whatever happened to be passing by.

✦ JOHN CALE
A Welshman and a student of composition, he moved to the United States, where he became acquainted with the works of minimalist avant-garde composers. He cofounded the Velvet Underground, along with Lou Reed.

✦ LOU REED
He studied English literature at Syracuse University with beat poet Delmore Schwartz, and became the brilliant, abrasive leader of the Velvet Underground in 1965.

WOODSTOCK

Between August 15 and 17, 1969, in Bethel, New York, 300,000 young people gathered from all over the United States for the rock festival that would be known to history as Woodstock, where it was originally supposed to take place. They spent three memorable days together, during which, in addition to listening to music, they lived the communal lifestyle according to the principles of the hippy movement— living peacefully side by side, sharing food, covers, and tents, and abandoning themselves to a drug-fueled daze. Woodstock seemed to predict a new type of society, made up of different kinds of people, guided by the leaders of the new, primarily California rock music, who were convinced more than ever that their music could change the world.

♦ JANIS JOPLIN
Janis Joplin, the alcohol- and drug-addicted white blues singer, offered memorable interpretations—passionate, sometimes aggressive, almost painful to listen to. She died in 1970.

♦ THE FESTIVAL PROGRAM
What is most striking when one runs down the list of artists who performed at Woodstock is their incredible variety. Country singers like Joe McDonald alternated with California rock groups such as the Jefferson Airplane, folk singers such as Joan Baez, and blues artists such as Janis Joplin. Their performances were not always memorable; the Grateful Dead, for example, did not go over especially well, while the then-unknown singer Joe Cocker caused a sensation with his rendition of the Beatles' "With a Little Help from My Friends." At a time when Eastern cultures were being widely explored, the performance by Indian musician Ravi Shankar was enthusiastically received. The presence of such British bands as The Who had great symbolic importance; it seemed to affirm the birth of a common rock culture. Above, the festival program.

♦ THE DOORS
The concert as a magical rite, where music is born of the direct contact between the artist and the public, was something that could not be achieved in the studio. This ideal found its most compelling exponent in Jim Morrison (above) of the Doors, a California group of the late 1960s.

♦ ORGANIZATION
Though conditions at Woodstock were difficult, there were no incidents, due in large part to the pacifist ideals upheld by the young audience, their use of drugs, and also to the organizing committee, led by hippies who were hard-working, helpful, and never intrusive.

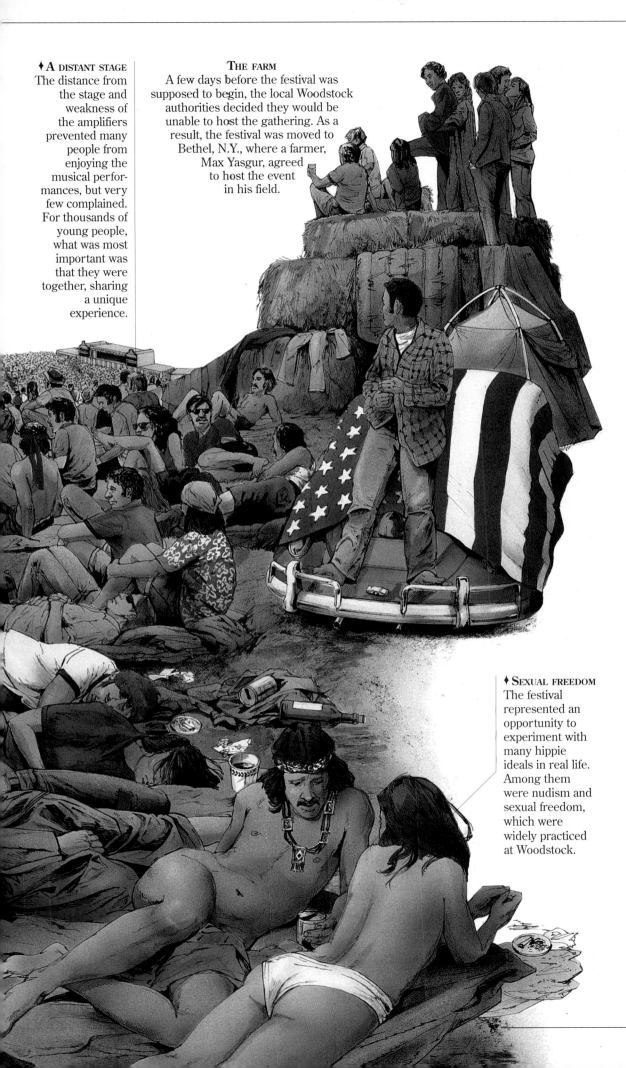

♦ A DISTANT STAGE
The distance from the stage and weakness of the amplifiers prevented many people from enjoying the musical performances, but very few complained. For thousands of young people, what was most important was that they were together, sharing a unique experience.

THE FARM
A few days before the festival was supposed to begin, the local Woodstock authorities decided they would be unable to host the gathering. As a result, the festival was moved to Bethel, N.Y., where a farmer, Max Yasgur, agreed to host the event in his field.

♦ THE GREAT ROCK FESTIVALS
Rock festivals had their beginnings, according to some, in the "trips festival" organized by Ken Kesey in January, 1966, when more than 6,000 people spent three days attending poetry readings, slide projections, and performances by rock groups. Others feel they began with the "Human Be-In" at San Francisco's Golden Gate Park Stadium on January 14, 1967, where painters, poets, play-wrights, and, above all, the major California rock bands, including the Grateful Dead and the Jefferson Airplane, took turns on stage. The most plausible date, however, is June 1967, with the Monterey, California festival. On that occasion, in the presence of 40,000 people, the marriage between the youth counter-culture and new rock music was officially celebrated. Above, a poster for the rock festival on the Isle of Wight in August 1970.

♦ SEXUAL FREEDOM
The festival represented an opportunity to experiment with many hippie ideals in real life. Among them were nudism and sexual freedom, which were widely practiced at Woodstock.

A DIRTY WAR

Having begun quietly during the Kennedy administration, the U.S. involvement in Vietnam intensified from 1965 on with aerial bombings of North Vietnam and the sending of ground troops into combat. Soon, however, the country was dismayed by the horrors of the war, and the impression that its true goal was not the freedom of the Vietnamese people but the defense of American interests. A movement against the conflict began to grow, led by pacifists and students. It became so large that by the end of the decade, it seemed the infernal war machine might actually be stopped. But the younger generation's hopes, exemplified by Woodstock, were dashed by the violence of some government leaders who did not hesitate to authorize the police to fire on university students in order to stop the protests.

♦ **THE ALTAMONT CONCERT (1969)**
The tense and sometimes violent climate in the country due to the war found its counterpart in the serious incidents at Altamont, California, during a Rolling Stones concert.

♦ **THE VIETNAM WAR**
U.S. military involvement in Vietnam—at that time divided into North and South Vietnam—was justified by the American government as necessary to stop the spread of Soviet influence throughout the world. To that end, from 1961 on, the United States sent arms and money to the South Vietnamese government, though it was an unpopular act and under attack from a national liberation front that favored unification with North Vietnam. Gradually, the U.S. government sent a number of military advisors, and finally, an army of nearly 500,000 troops in 1967. The American war machine, however, could not stop the South Vietnamese guerrillas who made a triumphant entry into Saigon in April 1975. Above, U.S. President Lyndon Johnson.

THE MARINES
A battalion of marines took part in a mopping-up operation in the South Vietnamese countryside, looking for Vietcong—partisans of the national liberation front.

♦ **THE KENT STATE UNIVERSITY INCIDENT**
In May 1970 the Ohio National Guard fired on Kent State University students who had been protesting sending American troops into Cambodia.

♦ **TELEVISION REPORTERS**
They documented the unheard-of violence inflicted on civilians by U.S. soldiers, which provoked disgust and opposition to the war among the American public.

**♦ THE
ENVIRONMENT**
One of the
reasons for the
U.S. defeat was
the hostile
environment of
tropical climates
and rain forests,
for which
American soldiers
were totally
unprepared.

**♦ THE NEW
PROTEST**
The reforms
passed by the
U.S. Congress in
1964 concerning
voting rights and
education for
African-Americans
had little impact
in reality. More
than half of
African-Americans
were unemployed
and living in
poverty, against
only 13 percent
of whites. From
the mid-1960s on,
the movement
for rights for
African-Americans
tended to
deemphasize
Martin Luther
King, Jr.'s
nonviolent
methods and to
encourage radical
forms of protest.
One of its most
charismatic
leaders was
Malcolm X
(above). The
movement
increasingly
focused on the
right to a separate
African-American
nation, in contrast
to the past quest
for integration
with whites. Riots
broke out in Los
Angeles in 1965,
killing thirty-four
people. Two years
later, forty-two
people died and
many more were
wounded in
Detroit's ghetto
revolt.

THE WAR
The casualty figures are horrifying:
more than 200,000 South Vietnamese
soldiers and an inestimable number of
civilians; more than 58,000 American
soldiers; and 24 million bombs dropped
on Vietnam, including napalm, which
can burn all living things in an
87-yard (80-m) radius.

**♦ THE ASSASSINATION OF
MARTIN LUTHER KING, JR.**
Martin Luther King, Jr., the leader in the
nonviolent struggle for civil rights, was
killed in Memphis, Tennessee, on April
4, 1968. His murder unleashed a wave of
violent protests in many American cities.

**♦ AFRICAN-AMERICAN
SOLDIERS**
Many African-
Americans were
sent to Vietnam.
With bitter irony,
Martin Luther King,
Jr. remarked that
they were going to
fight in Vietnam
for a freedom
they didn't enjoy
in Harlem.

THE ELECTRIC GENIUS

The electric guitar played a leading role in the history of rock and roll, from the early days of electric blues to Dylan's great transformation in 1965. It continued to do so through the end of the 1960s, thanks to the talent of Jimi Hendrix, a young African-American from Seattle. Hendrix had astonishing control over his guitar; he was able to reproduce practically any sound, and to create totally new ones, as well, thanks to recent technical advances. Hendrix, rebellious by nature and given to alcohol and drugs, was among the first artists to sense instinctively that the days of hope were coming to an end. His sound faithfully reflected this unease. Hendrix returned to old-style blues, transforming it into hard, angry, and deafening music, with extremely high levels of amplification.

♦ CREAM
Electronic blues, highly amplified, and close in style to Hendrix, was also the trademark of the supergroup Cream, founded in 1966 by Eric Clapton on electric guitar (above), Jack Bruce (bass), and George (Ginger) Baker (drums). Like Hendrix, the members of Cream boasted a technical mastery of their instruments that was almost unheard of in rock. The Beatles and the Rolling Stones were incomparable groups with a wealth of musical ideas, but they lacked exceptional instrumentalists; Cream, on the other hand, made technique their strong point. The group's breakup in 1968 did not mark the end of Eric Clapton's career; a true electric guitar virtuoso, he made outstanding contributions to other artists' musical projects and excelled in his own solo career.

IN MONTEREY
Hendrix ended his performance at the 1967 Monterey pop festival by setting fire to his guitar. The shocked spectators stared at the flames in horror, reminded of other, more dramatic fires.

♦ HIS PERFORMANCE
Hendrix indulged in an aggressive, highly theatrical style of performing, which was the key to his fame—along with his incomparable guitar technique. He played his guitar on the ground, behind his back, and even with his teeth.

♦ HIS GUITAR
Hendrix played a Stratocaster modified with the latest technological advances, including a "wah-wah" pedal.

♦ HIS CLOTHES

Hendrix's clothes were typical of the hippie movement, with which he was associated, as well as of psychedelia. His lyrics often made reference to drugs.

♦ AMPLIFIER

Hendrix created sound distortions by raising the volume of his amplifier. The result was a harsh, piercing tone, that Hendrix controlled masterfully.

♦ HENDRIX'S DEATH

His tragic death, like that of several rock stars, is shrouded in mystery. The official version has Hendrix dying in his sleep in London, on September 18, 1970, having suffocated in his own vomit following an overdose of tranquilizers. Above, his funeral.

♦ FENDER

As far back as the 1930s musicians used amplifiers to increase the volume of their guitars. It was Leo Fender (above), however, an engineer whose area of expertise was amplifier construction, who realized that electricity could be used to create a different quality of sound, and that electrification would allow musicians to manipulate the sound in previously unknown ways such as blending, reverberations, and tonal variations. He subsequently decided to build the first exclusively electric guitar that was sold starting in 1950 under the Telecaster brand name. His great breakthrough came two years later with a new model, the Stratocaster, which would become the inseparable companion of such rock heroes as Buddy Holly and Gene Vincent, and, with new technical enhancements, of Jimi Hendrix.

♦ HENDRIX AT WOODSTOCK

Jimi Hendrix closed the Woodstock festival (above, in performance). With his magical guitar he played a troubling and original version of the U.S. national anthem; the harsh, strident sound of the resonating strings carried the melody, while distortions and raps on the case reproduced the whistling and explosion of bombs.

THE DEVIL'S MUSIC

Between the 1960s and the 1970s came the birth and explosion of hard rock, a musical style that eventually became a separate genre—heavy metal—and that remains vital today. Hard rock also derives from the blues, but its sound is massive and original—songs open with tranquil, acoustic introductions, only to explode with highly distorted electric guitars, obsessive bass lines, and agonized voices, also distorted, all at an almost deafening volume. Hard rock is an attack on the rules of harmony by young people such as artists and audiences, who scorned bourgeois manners and who often indulged in violent, destructive behavior while listening to this music.

♦ **HARD ROCK AND TRANSVESTITISM**
Along with Led Zeppelin, such U.S. groups as MT and the Stooges took up a hard, deafening style of blues and created a vulgar, macho look to go along with their aggressive sounds. Soon, however, the heavy metal scene changed. In 1972 British singer David Bowie created Ziggy Stardust (above), an alien with a sexually ambiguous look, with both masculine and feminine traits, who conveyed a message of sexual nonconformity. For Bowie it was the start of a career marked by frequent changes in style; for hard rock in general, the explosion of a taste for sexual ambiguity that continues to this day. Subsequent groups, including Queen, played hard, distorted music in feminine clothes and heavy makeup.

AN ATTACK CONCERT
In the early 1970s Led Zeppelin, hard rock's most outstanding group, organized an "attack concert" along with fans in the parking lot of a mall.

SATANIC SYMBOLS
Hard rock also conveyed a passion for Satanism. Worshiping the devil—usually considered evil—was an outgrowth of a more generalized contempt for mainstream values and behavior.

♦ **FANS**
Led Zeppelin's aggressive behavior brought them fame; they were known for destroying hotel rooms, for example. Their fans were no less belligerent, and riots sometimes broke out during their concerts.

♦ **BLACK SABBATH**
This paragon of heavy metal groups was founded in 1969. Lead singer Ozzy Osborne was a true showman, and the group's crude and violent lyrics often provoked hostility in the media. Left, the cover of their first album, *Black Sabbath* (1970).

♦ **LED ZEPPELIN**
Founded in 1968 by guitarist Jimmy Page, Led Zeppelin is considered to be the father of hard rock. Throughout the 1970s their albums reached the top of the charts in the United States and Great Britain.

♦ **AMPLIFIERS**
Hard rockers raised the volume of their amplifiers to previously unimaginable levels. Their music sometimes came close to pure noise.

SINGER-SONGWRITERS

In the early 1970s rock was a success in record stores, though it had left behind its hopes for radical changes in society, and its most ambitious goals had gone unfulfilled. Record company profits were at an all-time high, and audiences continued to grow. Like all industries, however, the record industry eventually produced a series of nearly identical products. A new generation of singer-songwriters sprang up in the United States and contested this state of affairs. After a decade in which groups reigned supreme, these singer-songwriters were solitary figures who returned to the roots of American popular music: folk and country. They wrote songs that were simple from a musical point of view—but beautifully crafted—that told of unhappy love and private hopes and doubts, and that ceased to address larger social and political issues.

♦ **MARRIAGE IN CRISIS**
The attention paid by the new singer-song-writers, from Jackson Browne to Joni Mitchell (above), to the theme of solitude was born of the need to address a very real problem in contemporary American society: the breakdown of marriage. The number of divorces grew alarmingly in the 1970s, and by the end of the decade, three out of every five marriages ended in divorce. Adult men and women suddenly found themselves alone, grappling with emotional issues that had previously concerned only younger genera-tions. Most divorced people eventually remarried, but a growing number of Americans came to believe that marriage was an outdated institution and that the single life could be more fulfilling.

♦ **JACKSON BROWNE**
A native of California, he was one of the leaders of the country revival that characterized many singer-songwriters of his generation. In the mid-1970s his simple, direct lyrics won him great popularity.

A MOTEL
During a long, tiring 1971 tour, singer-songwriter James Taylor rested in a motel room.

♦ **LYRICS**
Spread out on the bed were pages filled with Taylor's lyrics. The lyrics were an extremely important element of his songs and of the works of all the new singer-songwriters. They told of love, pain, and friendship with great sensitivity.

MUSIC AND INDUSTRY
Though the new singer-songwriters often enjoyed excellent sales, they were critical of the record industry, which endlessly repeated the same old formulas and used the latest recording studio technologies to make up for a fundamental lack of new ideas.

♦ NIXON'S RESIGNATION
The early 1970s were marked by the resignation of Republican president Richard Nixon in 1974. Nixon had been implicated in the Watergate scandal, which involved spying on his Democratic political adversaries.

♦ GUITARS
The new generation of singer-song-writers returned to the simple sounds of the acoustic guitar, leaving behind the electronic distorted tones that had characterized the previous decade.

♦ HOLLYWOOD'S TURNING POINT
During the difficult years of the 1970s, the U.S. film industry, based in Hollywood, changed direction. The old formulas no longer worked— handsome actors and beautiful actresses, spectacular or emotionally vacuous stories, minimal contact with reality. Hollywood became dominated by such actors as Robert De Niro, Jack Nicholson, Al Pacino, Meryl Streep, and Dustin Hoffman; intense, gifted artists who had more to offer than just good looks. Scripts, too, were revolutionized, addressing current political and social themes such as the Vietnam War, Watergate, the Cold War, the breakdown of marriage, loneliness among adults, sexual freedom. Above, Robert De Niro in *Taxi Driver*.

♦ JAMES TAYLOR
A singer-songwriter and a superb guitarist with a warm, agreeable voice, his intense, delicate songs, including "Sweet Baby James" and "Fire and Rain," made him the leader of this new generation of musicians.

BEYOND ELVIS

Though the first signs had come a decade earlier as in the Beatles' experimental albums, for example, the 1970s saw many musicians, particularly in England, struggling to break free from rock and roll's traditions and to move popular music into new territories. Rock had been characterized by spontaneity, energy, and rhythm, but musicians now attempted to create complex, sophisticated music that sometimes seemed cold, and that was for listening rather than dancing. Western classical music helped inspire this new music; rock groups began collaborating with symphony orchestras. Live concerts in theaters with quiet, attentive audiences were soon outnumbered by elaborate sonic experiments carried out in recording studios.

♦ ROCK AND CLASSICAL MUSIC
Attempts to fuse rock with classical music were made possible by technological advances such as the invention of synthesizers, which allowed such 1970s British groups as Genesis, Jethro Tull, and Emerson, Lake, and Palmer to reproduce the sound of an orchestra's string section in the recording studio or in concert. Synthesizers allow for an enormously varied sound palette, and many musicians exaggerated their use, overburdening their songs with gratuitous sound effects. The new interest in classical music led many rock musicians to try to go beyond the traditional formal constraints of popular songs; they composed instrumental works that were comparable in length to symphonic movements. Above, the cover of *Fox Trot* by Genesis.

PINK FLOYD IN CONCERT
At Wembley Stadium in England, on November 16, 1974, the group Pink Floyd played the famous cut "Money" from their 1973 album *The Dark Side of the Moon*.

♦ LIGHT SHOWS
Light shows were an integral part of Pink Floyd's concerts. Technologically advanced and rehearsed down to the most minute details, they were perfectly synchronized with the music.

♦ MIXERS
Mixers took on a fundamental importance in Pink Floyd's concerts; they provided pre-recorded backgrounds for the group's music. Some of their songs included heartbeats, airplane sounds, explosions, and cash register noises.

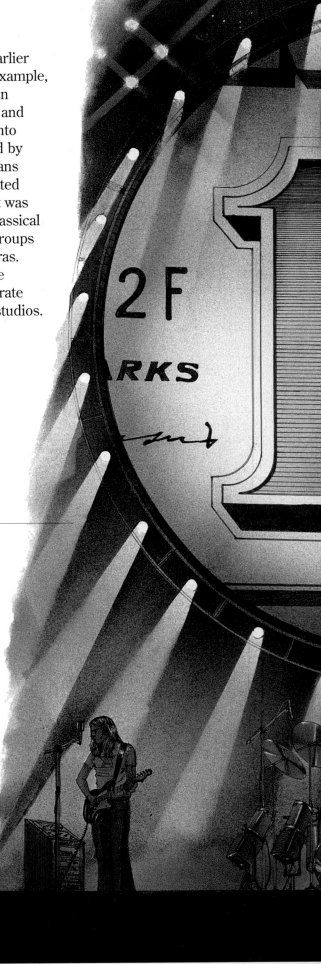

♦ THE CANTERBURY SCHOOL

This musical movement, born in the medieval town of Canterbury, England, explored the possible intersections of rock and jazz, even venturing forth into the most complex areas of classical music. Above, Robert Wyatt, leader of Soft Machine.

♦ PINK FLOYD

Founded in 1965, this group assumed a leading position in British psychedelia. In the 1970s, after the withdrawal of their leader, Syd Barret, Pink Floyd created a fascinating brand of music that combined orchestral interludes, sound effects, and folk ballads.

♦ THE CONCEPT ALBUM

The first concept album, in which all the songs had a thematic connection, or focused on the same basic story or situation, was the Beatles' *Sgt. Pepper*, followed by The Who's *Tommy* (1969). It wasn't until the 1970s, however, that the concept album really took off. Those interested in exploring connections with classical music were especially attracted by the possibilities of creating a musical structure lasting forty minutes, instead of the three minutes typical of rock songs. Jethro Tull, in particular, recorded *Thick as a Brick*, an ambitious work about a child prodigy's difficult life. Also notable were: *The Lamb Lies Down on Broadway* by Genesis and, at the end of the decade, *The Wall* by Pink Floyd (1979). Above, the album cover.

ANARCHY IN THE U.K.

The atmosphere was tense in mid-1970s London; the economy was in crisis, and youth unemployment was high. Many young people in Britain felt they had no future, and thus began to criticize the present. They rebelled against everyone and everything—the family, the state, religion, money—and proudly called themselves "punks." They used rock to give vent to their rage, an aggressive, savage, almost primitive form of rock, which shunned synthesizers and returned to the basic ensemble of rock's origins— guitar, bass, and drums. Their music was brought to life by guitars that played obsessively impossible rhythms and screaming voices.

♦ AFTER PUNK
Punk's most radical phase seemed to come to an end with the 1978 breakup of the Sex Pistols. The rage and violent attitudes of the earliest punks gave way to a no less troubling sense of defeat and resignation. In purely musical terms, punk gave way to "dark," which explored the themes of madness and of the inhumanity of modern society, enslaved by technology. Dark punk groups explored these themes with a frigid, remote vocal style and simple but obsessive rhythms. The Police, led by Sting, derived some of their energy from the punk movement; in 1978 they rose to the top of the charts with "Roxanne," combining punk's violence with the sweeter rhythms of Caribbean (reggae) music. Above, the dark group the Cure.

♦ CBGB
Shown above, the New York club where American punk emerged in the mid-1970s, following in the footsteps of the Velvet Underground with a mixture of rough rock and avant-garde literature and art. The great standard-bearers of American punk performed here, from Patti Smith (above) to the Ramones.

NO LIGHT SHOWS
Between 1975 and 1978 the Sex Pistols performed in cramped, intimate clubs. This choice was in defiance of the great technological shows of new rock, which punks considered servile to recording industry interests.

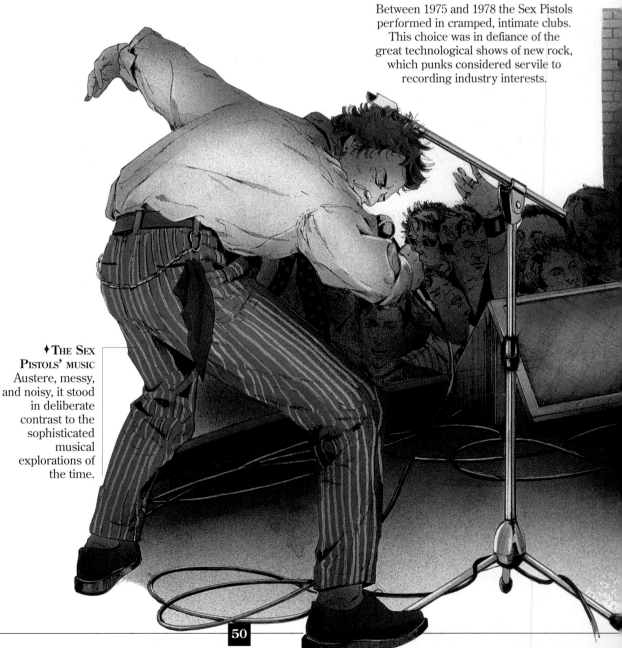

♦ THE SEX PISTOLS' MUSIC
Austere, messy, and noisy, it stood in deliberate contrast to the sophisticated musical explorations of the time.

♦ AUDIENCES
With pins stuck in their cheeks, torn pants, leather jackets, and brightly colored hair, their attitude was aggressive and mocking.

♦ THE SEX PISTOLS
This leading British punk group debuted in 1976 with the single "Anarchy in the U.K." Their contemptuous attitude, vulgar and belligerent language, and attacks on mainstream institutions caused hostility in traditionalists and racists alike.

♦ PUNK AND RECORD LABELS
The rise of punk, a spare, unadorned style of music and a spontaneous, homemade cultural product, gave new life to independent record labels that had been crushed by the majors, at the time the only labels that could withstand constantly rising production costs.

♦ THE 1970S
Throughout the decade, the western world suffered from an acute economic crisis, and suddenly found itself facing an energy crisis. In 1973 OPEC (the Organization of Petroleum-producing and Exporting Countries) quadrupled the price of crude oil, bringing about huge increases in the cost of transportation and industrial production. The United States, though suffering somewhat less from the energy crisis, was plagued with previously unheard-of unemployment levels. Furthermore, American leadership had been badly shaken by the U.S. defeat in Vietnam. Europe went through the same consequences in terms of unemployment, while certain countries—Italy and Germany among them—found their political stability threatened by violent acts of political terrorism. Above, an oil field.

♦ MALCOLM MCLAREN
The proprietor of an innovative London boutique, he became manager of the Sex Pistols in 1975. Provocative and intelligent, he promoted the punk phenomenon in the media.

VIDEO KILLED THE RADIO STAR

The reign of the video began and flourished in the 1980s. A new tool for promoting rock music, videos changed listeners' habits and ways of learning about music and had an enormous influence on both artists and record labels. Rich, seductive images relegated the music to the background—a basic law of perception where sight takes precedence over hearing. Though images had hardly been unimportant in rock's past, from the 1980s on, an attractive face or body became a prerequisite. Less talented artists often won fame thanks to carefully crafted videos, while more gifted singers sometimes struggled as actors in an effort to promote their music.

♦ MTV
Video's success also owed much to MTV, the first television channel to broadcast music videos twenty-four hours a day. Launched in 1981 by twenty-eight-year-old Robert Pittman, MTV almost immediately became the musical point of reference for young Americans. MTV launched such artists as Duran Duran and Spandau Ballet.

♦ "BOHEMIAN RHAPSODY"
The economic potential of combining video and music was seen for the first time in 1975 when Queen (above) reached the top of the charts after the BBC broadcast the images to accompany their song "Bohemian Rhapsody."

♦ FLASHDANCE
With its rapid, fragmentary images and pastel colors, the video also had an influence on movies; one example is Adrian Lyne's *Flashdance* (1983) with Jennifer Beals.

♦ "THRILLER"
Video's potential for promoting a musician's work became clear with Michael Jackson's tremendously successful video "Thriller" (1983).

♦ A NEW LANGUAGE
Video was most appealing to young audiences, who had grown up with televison and were quick to understand its visual language.

TOKYO
In a Tokyo street, teenagers went wild for videos shown on outdoor screens.

✦ **MADONNA**
The goddess of 1980s music, she used videos to highlight her talents as a sexy singer, dancer, and actress.

✦ **MICHAEL JACKSON**
Michael Jackson, the leading dance-music artist of the 1980s, was the first to use videos to conquer the world market.

VIDEOS
Videos gave record labels the huge advantage of being able to launch a song on a worldwide scale without having to spend a fortune sending artists on tour.

✦ **THE 1980s**
The decade opened with the election of Ronald Reagan. Reagan's presidency, driven by a conservative vision of the world—family, law and order, and patriotism and economic libertarianism, with no limits on competition—set the tone for the decade. Success, money, and personal development were the keywords of the day. In the meantime, events in the Soviet Union would have momentous consequences. In 1985 the new Soviet leader Mikhail Gorbachev introduced democratic reforms into the Soviet system and helped bring about the end of the Cold War with the West. His choices were dictated in part by serious internal problems, and eventually led to the demolition of the Berlin Wall in 1989 (above) and to the rebirth of liberty for the people of Eastern Europe.

✦ **COMPACT DISCS**
The compact disc was launched during the 1980s. It is a digital medium that converts the thousands of information bits recorded on it into sound. It offers good sound quality and is much more sturdy than vinyl.

A TECHNOLOGICAL REVOLUTION

♦ **1980s**
TECHNO-POP
The video age saw the rise of techno-pop, especially in England, electronic music with a dance beat. Techno-pop revolved around the synthesizer, which made traditional bands such as rhythmic and solo guitar, bass, and drums, obsolete and gave rise to many duos consisting of an electronic keyboard player and a solo singer. These included Yazoo, whose member Alison Moyet later had a brilliant solo career, and, a few years later, the Pet Shop Boys (above). Duran-Duran and Spandau Ballet were also techno-pop groups; they created unique looks, both elegant and eccentric, to go with their vaguely electronic dance music.

The rock world has always had a love-hate relationship with technology. When rock was young, the then futuristic electric guitar led to enthusiasm but also suspicion. The same thing happened with electronic keyboards in the 1970s. This was nothing, however, in comparison with the fears and passions awakened in the 1980s with the introduction of increasingly sophisticated synthesizers and, above all, of samplers, machines that could record any sound and manipulate it in real time according to the musician's needs. Samplers changed music making itself. Infinite tonal possibilities were available to anyone who felt like composing, with or without talent or knowledge of music theory.

♦ **LAURIE ANDERSON**
She was an American artist who combined theater, dance, and painting, and used fascinating electronic music in multimedia works. With her 1982 album *O Superman*, she found herself unexpectedly at the top of the British charts.

♦ **AN ATTORNEY**
Among other duties, the attorney addresses the issue of whether brief formulas or sound fragments taken from one recording and used in a different, original work represent a violation of copyright.

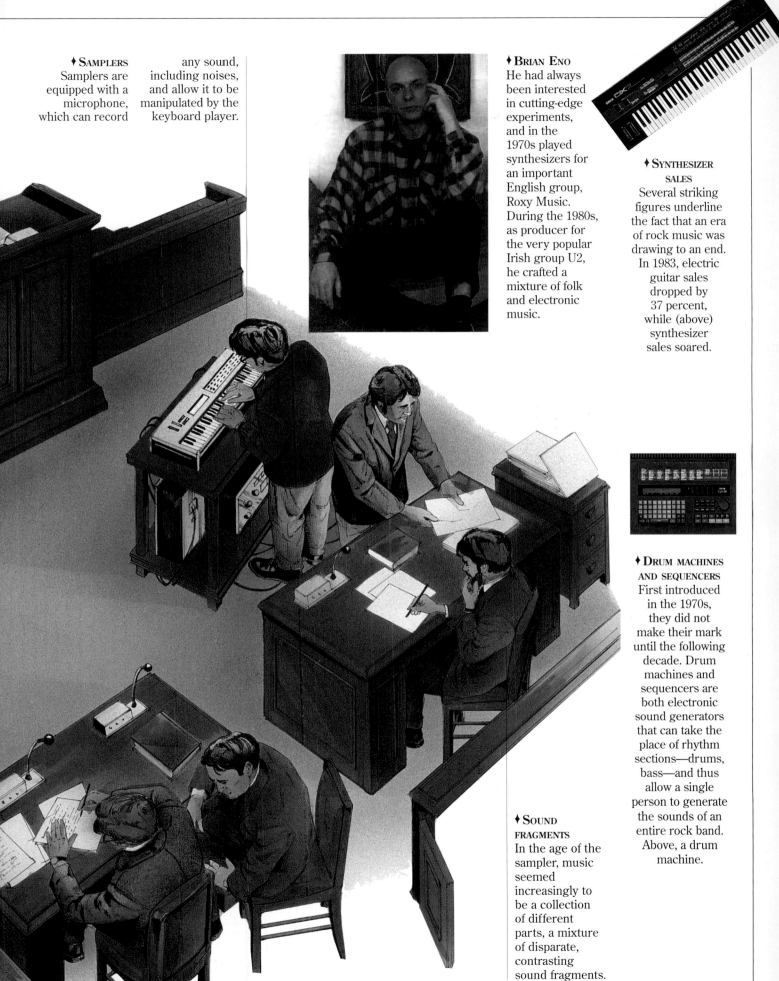

♦ **SAMPLERS**
Samplers are equipped with a microphone, which can record any sound, including noises, and allow it to be manipulated by the keyboard player.

♦ **BRIAN ENO**
He had always been interested in cutting-edge experiments, and in the 1970s played synthesizers for an important English group, Roxy Music. During the 1980s, as producer for the very popular Irish group U2, he crafted a mixture of folk and electronic music.

♦ **SYNTHESIZER SALES**
Several striking figures underline the fact that an era of rock music was drawing to an end. In 1983, electric guitar sales dropped by 37 percent, while (above) synthesizer sales soared.

♦ **DRUM MACHINES AND SEQUENCERS**
First introduced in the 1970s, they did not make their mark until the following decade. Drum machines and sequencers are both electronic sound generators that can take the place of rhythm sections—drums, bass—and thus allow a single person to generate the sounds of an entire rock band. Above, a drum machine.

♦ **SOUND FRAGMENTS**
In the age of the sampler, music seemed increasingly to be a collection of different parts, a mixture of disparate, contrasting sound fragments.

BORN TO RUN

By the mid-1980s the invasion of electronic and digital instruments and the great success of videos caused some young people to seek out a more "authentic" type of music, with the vitality of traditional rock and roll. Bruce Springsteen, known as "the Boss," best embodied this trend. Springsteen's enormous popularity was built on his concert appearances, not on studio recordings. More than anything else, he returned to rock's musical roots of rhythm and blues and 1950s rock and roll, singing of timeless passions such as cars, women, freedom, and escape, but also of America's cruel realities of unemployment and marginalized people.

IN CONCERT
Bruce Springsteen about to begin one of the concerts of his triumphant 1984–85 *Born in the U.S.A.* tour.

♦ **U2 AND R.E.M.**
The legacy of "genuine" rock was taken up in the 1980s by Springsteen and by two groups, U2 and R.E.M. (above). The makeup of their bands—vocals, solo guitar, bass, and drums—was revealing in itself; a return to the traditional rock ensemble and its classic sounds. U2's first two albums, in fact (*Boy* and *War*), combined energy, toughness, and innocence, a mixture that would characterize their musical world even after their collaborations with the innovative Brian Eno. More self-conscious and polished than U2, R.E.M.'s style, though richer and different in many respects from classic rock, especially because of their leader's unique vocals, also reflected the influence of traditional rock. R.E.M.'s first great popular success came in 1988, with their album *Document* (1987).

♦ **THE E-STREET BAND**
Springsteen's ensemble band reflected his music's roots, from Clarence Clemons' rhythm and blues sax to the 1950s rock-style piano of Danny Federici.

♦ **SPRINGSTEEN**
A true rock hero who conveyed incredible energy in his concerts, Springsteen was nevertheless different in many respects from traditional rockers—no drinking, drugs, or excessive lifestyles.

♦ **BORN TO RUN**
With his 1975 album *Born to Run*, Springsteen climbed to the top of the charts for the first time and made the cover of *Newsweek* magazine.

♦ **A TIME OF COMMITMENT**
The second half of the 1980s saw rock awash in a wave of altruism. In contrast to the 1960s, however, 1980s rock did not seek to tear down traditional institutions but simply to improve them. At the initiative of singer Bob Geldof (above), who had been horrified by a BBC program on the Ethiopian famine, Britain's musical stars gathered to make a benefit recording. Similar events followed, the most important of which was "Live Aid" (July 13, 1985), a series of concerts in London and Philadelphia that raised funds for world hunger and that, like Woodstock, brought together all the different strands of rock, from Madonna and Bob Dylan to the Rolling Stones and Sting.

♦ **HIS GUITAR**
Springsteen once said of himself, "I'm the man with the guitar." He played both electric rock guitar and acoustic folk guitar, sometimes separately, sometimes combining the two styles.

THE GHETTO BEAT

Rap music was born in the 1970s and exploded in the 1980s, thanks to the creative power of the African-American community, its magnificent musical traditions, and its struggles in the ghettoes of urban America. A rap song is based on a sampling of some other musical fragment, such as a short guitar melody, for example, repeated almost obsessively and enriched with a drum machine and half-sung declamations. Strong rhythms accompany harsh descriptions of ghetto realities of drugs, youth gangs, and poverty, denunciations of racial discrimination, and expressions of pride in African-American identity.

♦ RAP HISTORY
Though its roots go far back—to blues and African music—rap was born in the 1970s when deejays introduced Jamaican "dub" music to New York. It combined declamation with a reggae (Jamaican) musical base. Dub failed to take off, but the basic idea caught on, and deejay Kool Herc replaced reggae with funk rhythms, which captivated young people. Kool Herc, Grandmaster Flash, and Afrika Bambaataa (above) were some of rap's outstanding deejays and created the fundamentals of the new musical style, such as "scratching." They were soon hired to perform in New York's leading discos and attracted a growing number of young African-American fans. The independents soon developed an interest in rap, and in 1979 the Sugarhill Gang recorded "Rapper's Delight," the first rap song to reach the top of the charts.

♦ TUPAC SHAKUR
One of the most famous and troubled rappers, Shakur was arrested many times and died in Las Vegas in 1996, shot down by unknown assailants.

GHETTO LIFE
A rap party in Harlem, New York's African-American neighborhood. Rap was born in ghetto streets and underground clubs, the legacy of restless young African-Americans.

♦ MC
The figure of the MC (or "Master of Ceremonies") emerged. He recited poetry over the music, while deejays were free to concentrate on their own creative work.

RHYTHM
Rap brought back to popular music that "danceable" quality that rock had gradually deemphasized.

♦ DEEJAYS
Rap does not require a traditional band, just a deejay with some turntables, a sampler, and a drum machine. The deejay appropriates a small fragment of someone else's record and repeats it *ad infinitum*, with the drum machine providing accompaniment.

♦ PRINCE
In Prince, the Minneapolis-born artist whose album *Purple Rain* enjoyed great popularity, African-American music found an extraordinary musical personality who brought together an extremely innovative sound palette, an unprecedented use of harmony and vital, energetic rhythms. He would later use a symbol for his name.

♦ SCRATCHING
Deejays pushed records back and forth, with the record needle creating a scratching sound.

♦ GRAFFITI
Rap is connected to some of the other art forms of African-American youth, notably graffiti, painted on walls and subway cars.

♦ RAP AND CENSORSHIP
Throughout the 1980s cuts in government spending had a terrible effect on the lives of young African-Americans. High levels of unemployment in the inner cities led to drug pushing and gangs. Rap from California, known as "gangsta rap," told about all aspects of these new realities using crude language, and sometimes expressing admiration for such figures as drug dealers or gang leaders. Parents' associations and fundamentalist religious groups attacked gangsta rap and sometimes managed to have it banned from the airwaves, or at least to have profane language "bleeped" out.

GRUNGE

Rock sometimes slows down as if to catch its breath, only to be reborn with fresh energy. This was the case in the early 1990s with groups such as Nirvana and Pearl Jam, from Seattle and surrounding areas. Their music is hard to define, combining punk—fast electric guitar playing—heavy metal, with its deafening volumes, as well as a melodic vein similar to the Beatles (in the case of Nirvana). After cutting their teeth in underground clubs, these groups offered a new musical style, called "grunge," as well as an innovative look and unconventional behavior. Their songs stood out for their dark, hopeless atmosphere and stories of failure and of paranoia, all too familiar to troubled young generations.

♦ PUNK AND A NEW GENERATION
Grunge's music and lyrics were inspired by the wave of punk or hardcore California bands that included the Black Flags and the Dead Kennedys (above), who attracted a following among those young people who still believed in rock as a militant, rebellious musical form. Punk's survival as a harsh, aggressive musical form represented young people's response to a reality that they found intolerable—that is, that their hateful, distant parents had also grown up with rock and had loved it. Rock had to become brutal, "unlistenable" noise so that adults would stay away from it. For similar reasons, a variation of heavy metal known as "thrash" exploded in the mid-1980s. Its most successful band was Metallica.

♦ BJÖRK
The Icelandic singer Björk emerged in the early 1990s, offering a musical style somewhere between avant-garde explorations and a return to traditional musical forms.

♦ NIRVANA
They were: Kurt Cobain (electric guitar), Chris Novoselic (bass), and Dave Grohl (drums). After their earliest recordings for Sub Pop, they signed with Geffen and recorded *Nevermind* (1992), an album that rose to the top of the national charts.

♦ **KURT COBAIN**
He was lead vocalist for Nirvana and the musical soul of the group. Depressed and addicted to heroin, he committed suicide on April 6, 1994.

Sub Pop

♦ **SUB POP**
Grunge's great success owed much to an independent Seattle label, Sub Pop Records, established in 1986 by a former deejay, Bruce Pavitt. He signed up some of the major grunge groups, including Nirvana and Soundgarden, and also managed to draw the mass media's attention to Seattle and its new musical scene.

♦ **NEW DIRECTIONS**
Another interesting phenomenon of the 1990s rock world was the discovery or rediscovery of world ethnic and popular music. Such artists as David Byrne and Peter Gabriel (above) began to develop the fascinating idea of combining traditional world music with more modern sounds.

♦ **GRUNGE STYLE**
Nirvana, Pearl Jam, and Soundgarden also created a grunge style consisting of long hair, flannel shirts or T-shirts, torn jeans, and sneakers or low boots.

CHRONOLOGY

1951 Alan Freed, deejay at WJW, Cleveland, uses the term "rock and roll" for the first time in his show's title. Senator McCarthy's Communist witch-hunt continues.

1954 "Sh-boom" by the Crew Cuts becomes the first rhythm and blues song to hit the top ten. Elvis makes his first official recording in Memphis's Sun studios.

1955 "Rock Around the Clock" by Bill Haley and the Comets is the first rock and roll song to hit number one on the pop charts. Chuck Berry records "Maybelline"; Little Richard records "Tutti Frutti."

1956 With "Hound Dog," his first RCA single, Elvis hits number one on the pop, country and western, and rhythm and blues charts. "Presleymania" erupts all over the United States.

1959 Buddy Holly dies in a plane crash, along with Ritchie Valens and others. Chuck Berry is accused of statutory rape. The payola scandal erupts. Elvis does his military service at a U.S. base in West Germany.

1960 The Beatles perform for the first time in Hamburg, Germany. John Fitzgerald Kennedy is elected president of the United States.

1961 Robert Zimmerman, known as Bob Dylan, performs for the first time at Folk City, a Greenwich Village club. Kennedy sends the first U.S. troops to Vietnam.

1963 The Beatles record "Please Please Me." Another British group takes the name the Rolling Stones. Martin Luther King, Jr. leads the march on Washington. President Kennedy is assassinated; Lyndon Johnson becomes president.

1964 The Beatles arrive in the United States to a hysterical welcome. In San Francisco the Warlocks (later known as the Grateful Dead) start performing.

1965 Dylan is booed at the Newport Folk Festival. He records the album *Highway 61 Revisited*, which includes the historic cut "Like a Rolling Stone." The Rolling Stones record "I Can't Get No (Satisfaction)."

1967 The Beatles' *Sgt. Pepper* and Jimi Hendrix's *Are You Experienced?* come out. The first Monterey festival takes place. There are race riots in several U.S. cities.

1968 Led Zeppelin debuts. The Tet offensive starts in Vietnam. Martin Luther King, Jr. is assassinated in Memphis. Student riots break out all over Europe, inspired by those in the United States.

1969 One of the most important gatherings in rock history—known as Woodstock—takes place in Bethel, New York on Max Yasgur's farm. The Rolling Stones give a tumultuous concert at Altamont.

1970 The Beatles officially split up. Jimi Hendrix and Janis Joplin die. The U.S. National Guard and Kent State University students clash.

1973 Pink Floyd releases *The Dark Side of the Moon*, an album that would sell an unprecedented thirteen million copies. OPEC quadruples the price of crude oil, leading to the energy crisis.

1975 Patti Smith releases *Horses*. The Vietcong enter Saigon, capital of South Vietnam. The Vietnam War comes to an end.

1976 The Sex Pistols release their first single, "Anarchy in the U.K." Bruce Springsteen's success grows with *Born to Run*.

1979 The first rap single hits the charts—"Rapper's Delight" by the Sugarhill Gang. Pink Floyd's album *The Wall* is released.

1980 John Lennon is murdered. R.E.M. debuts; their first major success is *Document* (1987). Ronald Reagan is elected president of the United States.

1982 Michael Jackson's album *Thriller* comes out. The compact disc is launched. The MTV channel, founded a year earlier, broadcasts twenty-four hours a day.

1984 Springsteen releases *Born in the U.S.A.* and undertakes one of the most successful tours in rock history.

1985 "Live Aid," a concert relayed between London and Philadelphia, raises funds for world hunger. Mikhail Gorbachev is nominated head of the Soviet Communist party.

1987 U2's album *The Joshua Tree* hits number one all over the world. R.E.M.'s album *Document* is released. Nirvana debuts.

1991 Nirvana releases *Nevermind*, which would eventually sell ten million copies. Metallica's album *Metallica* is released.

1994 Kurt Cobain, the leader of Nirvana, commits suicide. The debut album by Icelandic singer Björk, *Debut* (1993), attracts critical and popular attention.

1995 The Rock and Roll Hall of Fame and Museum opens in Cleveland, Ohio, and features costumes and instruments used by rock music performers, original song manuscripts, and films showing rock music performances and history.

DISCOGRAPHY

Recommended listening follows for many of the spreads in this book, recordings that will give a more complete understanding of the issues under discussion. Solo albums and CDs are emphasized, since 45 rpm discs have virtually disappeared from the market.

ORIGINS
MUDDY WATERS, *The Best of Muddy Waters* (Chess, 1958).
HOWLIN' WOLF, *Moanin' in the Moonlight*, 1951–57 (Chess, 1958).
FATS DOMINO, *Rock and Rollin' with Fats Domino* (Imperial, 1956) and the first two volumes of his complete recordings: *Story*, Vol. 1—*The Fat Man* (United Artists, 1977) and *Story* Vol. 2—*Ain't That a Shame* (United Artists, 1977).

THE NEW MUSIC ARRIVES
BILL HALEY AND THE COMETS, *Rock Around the Clock*, 33 rpm (Decca, 1955).

INDEPENDENT LABELS
CHUCK BERRY, *After School Session* (Chess, 1957); *One Dozen Berries* (Chess, 1958); *Berry Is on Top* (Chess, 1959).

ELVIS: THE KING
ELVIS PRESLEY, *Elvis Presley* (RCA, 1956); *Elvis* (RCA, 1956); *Loving You* (RCA, 1957); *Elvis Christmas Album* (RCA, 1957); *Jailhouse Rock* (RCA, 1958).

THE HOWL
LITTLE RICHARD, *His Biggest Hits* (Specialty, 1963).
JERRY LEE LEWIS, *Jerry Lee Lewis* (Sun, 1958).

PRIVATE PRESLEY
BUDDY HOLLY, *The Complete Buddy Holly* (MCA, 1979)
RITCHIE VALENS, *La Bamba* (45 rpm) (Delfi, 1958).

MY NAME IS BOB DYLAN
BOB DYLAN, *Bob Dylan* (Columbia, 1962); *The Freewheelin'* (Columbia, 1963); *Highway 61 Revisited* (Columbia, 1965); THE BYRDS, *Mr. Tambourine Man* (Columbia, 1965).

THE FAB FOUR
THE BEATLES, *Please Please Me* (Parlophone, 1963); *With the Beatles* (Parlophone, 1963); *A Hard Day's Night* (Parlophone, 1964); *Help!* (Parlophone, 1965).

THE NEW BAD BOYS
THE ROLLING STONES, *The Rolling Stones* (Decca, 1964); *The Rolling Stones* (Decca, 1965); *Out of Our Heads* (Decca, 1965); *Aftermath* (Decca, 1966).
THE WHO, *My Generation* (Brunswick, 1965).

MARCHING FORWARD
JAMES BROWN, *Live at the Apollo* (King, 1963); *Papa's Got a Brand New Bag* (King, 1965).
OTIS REDDING, *Complete & Unbelievable— The Otis Redding Dictionary of Soul*, 1966 (Volt, 1967).

THE SUMMER OF LOVE
THE GRATEFUL DEAD, *Grateful Dead* (Warner Bros., 1967).
KEN KESEY, *The Acid Trip* (Sound City, 1967).
THE JEFFERSON AIRPLANE, *Surrealistic Album* (RCA, 1967).
THE BEACH BOYS, *Surfin' USA* (Capitol, 1963).

A HISTORIC ALBUM
THE BEATLES, *Revolver* (Parlophone, 1966); *Sgt. Pepper's Lonely Hearts Club Band* (Parlophone, 1967); *The Beatles* (*White Album*) (Apple, 1968).

ROCK IN THE GALLERIES
THE VELVET UNDERGROUND & NICO, *The Velvet Underground & Nico* (Verve, 1967).
FRANK ZAPPA, *We're Only in It for the Money* (Verve, 1968).

WOODSTOCK
THE DOORS, *The Doors* (Elektra, 1967).
BIG BROTHER & THE HOLDING COMPANY (JANIS JOPLIN), *Sex, Dope & Cheap Thrills* (Mainstream, 1967).
VARIOUS, *Woodstock* (Cotillon, 1970) three LPs.

THE ELECTRIC GENIUS
JIMI HENDRIX, *Are You Experienced?* (Polydor, 1967); *The Essential*, Vol. 1 (Reprise, 1978); and *The Essential*, Vol. 2 (Reprise, 1980).

THE DEVIL'S MUSIC
LED ZEPPELIN, *Led Zeppelin* (Atlantic, 1969); *Led Zeppelin II* (Atlantic, 1969); and *Led Zeppelin III* (Atlantic, 1970); *Presence* (Swansong, 1976).
BLACK SABBATH, *Sabbath Bloody Sabbath* (Vertigo, 1973).
QUEEN, *A Night at the Opera* (EMI, 1975).
DAVID BOWIE, *The Rise and Fall of Ziggy Stardust and the Spiders from Mars* (RCA, 1972).

SINGER-SONGWRITERS
JAMES TAYLOR, *Sweet Baby James* (Warner Bros, 1970).
JACKSON BROWNE, *Running on Empty* (Asylum, 1977).
JONI MITCHELL, *For the Roses* (Asylum, 1972).

BEYOND ELVIS
EMERSON, LAKE, & PALMER, *Pictures at an Exhibition* (Island/Help, 1971).
GENESIS, *The Lamb Lies Down on Broadway* (Charisma, 1974).
PINK FLOYD, *The Dark Side of the Moon* (Harvest, 1973); *The Wall* (Harvest, 1979).
THE WHO, *Tommy* (Track, 1969).

ANARCHY IN THE U.K.
THE SEX PISTOLS, *Never Mind the Bollocks, Here's the Sex Pistols* (Virgin, 1977).
THE CLASH, *Clash* (CBS, 1977).
THE RAMONES, *Ramones* (Sire, 1976).
PATTI SMITH, *Horses* (Arista, 1975).
THE CURE, *Seventeen Seconds* (Fiction, 1980).
THE POLICE, *Outlandos d'Amour* (A&M, 1978).

VIDEO KILLED THE RADIO STAR
MICHAEL JACKSON, *Thriller* (Epic, 1982).
MADONNA, *Like a Virgin* (Sire, 1984).

A TECHNOLOGICAL REVOLUTION
LAURIE ANDERSON, *Home of the Brave* (Warner Bros., 1986).
BRIAN ENO & DAVID BYRNE, *My Life in the Bush of Ghosts* (EB, 1981).

BORN TO RUN
BRUCE SPRINGSTEEN, *Born to Run* (Columbia, 1975); *Born in the U.S.A.* (Columbia, 1984).
U2, *The Joshua Tree* (Island, 1987).
R.E.M., *Document* (I.R.S., 1987).

THE GHETTO BEAT
PUBLIC ENEMY, *Apocalypse 91...the Enemy Strikes Black* (Def Jam, 1991).
RUN-DMC, *Together Forever, (Greatest Hits 1983–1998).* (FPR Profile, 1999).

GRUNGE
NIRVANA, *Nevermind* (Sub Pop/DGC, 1991); *MTV Unplugged in New York* (DGC, 1994).
DEAD KENNEDYS, *In God We Trust, Inc.* (Alternative Tentacle, 1981).
METALLICA, *Kill 'em All* (Megaforce, 1983).
BJÖRK, *Debut* (One Little Iindian, 1993).
DAVID BYRNE, *Feelings* (Luaka Bop/Warner Bros., 1997).

INDEX